Language for Life

This new edition of the bestselling *Language for Life* shows how language can be mastered by children and how what they have learned can be carried throughout their lives.

An indispensable guidebook for teachers, it delivers explicit, step-by-step English language instruction via lessons in syntax, grammar, morphology, etymology, and punctuation, and arms students with the mental skill of thinking about language. This in turn helps children learn much more easily from the language around them. New features for this edition include:

- an increased focus on the relationship between knowledge of parts of speech and morphology to proficiency as a writer
- creating a metalanguage between student and teacher that encourages clear two-way feedback
- an increased focus on knowledge-building using factual topics as exemplars.

Language for Life is a proven program that is built upon years of experience. Lyn Stone's pragmatic and modern approach is supported by feedback from teachers and students alike who have attended her numerous classes and workshops. This book helps teachers: learn more about language structure, guide the development of skills to write accurately and in increasing volume, and support the emergence of clear and organised thinking for writing.

Brimming with vital information suitable for both basic and advanced level students, this book is an essential tool for all teachers wishing to give their students the best preparation possible to meet the demands of the modern world. Photocopiable worksheets throughout the book put teachers in the position of linguistic expert, guiding students through an enriching journey of language discovery and creativity.

Lyn Stone is an educational linguist based in Australia. She is the owner of Lifelong Literacy, a specialist tutoring practice and teacher training institute. She and her team provide online courses and in-person coaching to educators across the globe.

Language for Life

Where Linguistics Meets Teaching

Second Edition

Lyn Stone

Routledge
Taylor & Francis Group

LONDON AND NEW YORK

Designed cover image: Jo Steer

Second edition published 2025
by Routledge
4 Park Square, Milton Park, Abingdon, Oxon, OX14 4RN

and by Routledge
605 Third Avenue, New York, NY 10158

Routledge is an imprint of the Taylor & Francis Group, an informa business

First edition published by Routledge 2016

British Library Cataloguing-in-Publication Data
A catalogue record for this book is available from the British Library

ISBN: 978-1-032-60178-6 (hbk)
ISBN: 978-1-032-60177-9 (pbk)
ISBN: 978-1-003-45793-0 (ebk)

DOI: 10.4324/9781003457930

Typeset in Helvetica
by Apex CoVantage, LLC

Contents

Figures

Acknowledgements

I remain indebted to Dick Hudson, Professor of Linguistics (Emeritus) UCL, a man who has quietly and gently done a great deal to promote the teaching of linguistics in schools. Despite being many years retired, he still found time to immediately answer any queries I sent him.

I must also thank the infinitely witty Professor Anatoly Liberman, another scholar who never failed to answer my emails, be they calls for clarification, interview appearances in my online Language Arts Course, or requests to poach his beautifully crafted sentences. I still avidly read his OUP Blog, entitled *The Oxford Etymologist*, and consider him the etymologist's etymologist.

Etymology has reached into education through the efforts of people like Hudson and Liberman, but a relatively new resource, *The Online Etymology Dictionary*, compiled by Douglas Harper, has taken the study of words and their stories to new heights. My thanks go to Doug for his incredible work and for permission to share his insights.

Numerous kind and patient scholars have advised me over the years leading up to this second edition. Among them are the late and very sorely missed William Van Cleave, the clear-thinking and very kind Kylie Conrad, and the inimitable Jasmine Shannon.

I have also had the pleasure of working alongside many dedicated and hardworking team-members at my tutoring practice, one of whom in particular, Amanda Bugiera, has been the most loyal and entertaining companion. The team have spent years field-testing my resources, and pushing their development to ever-increasing heights.

My girls are now women and making their mark on the world. Brought up by a mum who becomes very forgetful and distracted around book deadline time, they have not only supported me merely by existing, but in so many other ways too. They are the lights of my life.

It would be remiss of me not to acknowledge my kind and patient publishers, Routledge. Once again they have given me the opportunity to bring my works up to a higher standard and to a wider audience.

Foreword

As the old joke goes, 'There are three types of people in this world: those who can count and those who can't.' I lean towards being in the second category. In response to the derision I sometimes receive from those in the *can* category, I say, 'Those are numbers. I do words.'

I have been thinking and talking about words as both an occupation and a preoccupation for over thirty years. When I talk to my students about words, I get the impression that they need to know certain things, and that if I teach them in a certain way, they are likely to remember and use those things in life.

This is how *Language for Life* came about. The main features of the book are:

- lessons for students
- knowledge for teachers
- resources for everyone.

When I was teaching grammar, questions about morphology and punctuation inevitably arose. In response, I began compiling teaching materials from relevant resources, which I then used to develop programs of learning.

After testing these lessons and resources, I began to offer them as teacher-training workshops. It was then that I discovered another set of facts: teachers needed to attain a better knowledge of language, and if this knowledge was conveyed in a particular way, they were likely to remember and use that knowledge in their own teaching.

This new edition has been updated to reflect my current understanding of syntax and morphology and how best to bring others to a similar understanding. For that reason I've expunged the more advanced phrase-structure trees and lengthened the updated list of word-forming elements.

Another major change in this edition is that instead of using example words and sentences based on people I know, I have chosen seven of my favourite birds. This reflects my change in understanding about the importance of building knowledge with students wherever possible. It's a form of practising what I preach to the teachers who come to my training. Each bird I have personally encountered and have a great deal of admiration for. You never forget the first time you met a brolga.

Finally, I have found over the years that my students enjoyed it when I personified the parts of speech and likened them to people living together in a busy city. As a result, I have had each major word category illustrated and I wrote a paragraph about each one.

How to use this book

The lesson sections of this book are supported by face-to-face and online courses as well as by a growing set of free YouTube videos.

This book is intended to be descriptive, while offering a range of essential facts about language and learning, with a focus on grammar and syntax.

Figure 0.1 sets out all the major parts of speech, their markings, and their relationships in one diagram. Please refer to it when introducing a new concept, and when you are going about review. It may look complex at first,

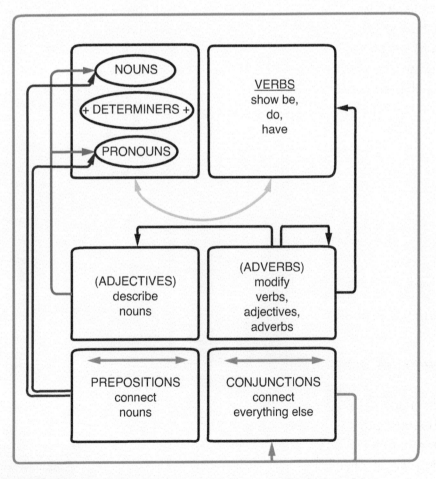

Figure 0.1 Parts of speech, their markings, and relationships

but as you go through the program, it starts to make sense. Please don't overwhelm your students by asking them to interpret it at the outset of your syntax lessons.

Using a simple marking system and a set of knowledge-building example sentences, each lesson tells the story of a different part of speech. The marking system graphically illustrates the relationships the words have to one another as we tell the stories.

I have used the subject of birds to provide examples of words, phrases, sentences, and clauses throughout the book. As the teacher, you can use any subject, but I do recommend that you try to build general knowledge as you go. My suggestion would be to use examples from subjects being studied in other lessons. For instance, a common topic in primary school is the weather. Instead of *The dog runs*, you could use something like *The clouds gather*. Small tweaks like that make big changes over time.

In this analysis, we connect words to one another with a range of arrows and lines to show their relationships. In the example paragraphs, sometimes a word will be separated from another word by a line break. In this instance, we draw a line from the first word to the end of the line, then a dot to act as an anchor point, a dot at the beginning of the next line, and we continue the drawn line until it reaches its destination word (see Figure 0.2).

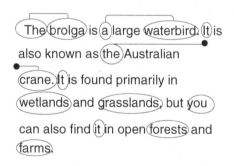

Figure 0.2 Pronoun example passage marked

How to use the suggested scope and sequence

Each year level is split into a number of weeks of focus activities. We begin at the foundation year, that is, the first year of formal schooling. It is referred to in a number of ways across the globe, so what is meant is the first year during which children attend full-time school and begin to learn to read and write.

The foundation year is about orally introducing concepts to lay the groundwork for the coming lessons. It is a good idea to have your whole school or district using this scope and sequence to ensure continuity. Grammar, syntax, and morphology aren't mastered in a year.

In recommendations and principles deriving from cognitive load theory, there is an effect known as *transience*. It was originally coined to describe the increase in extraneous cognitive load when information that students need disappears (e.g. in slideshows or discussions) and forces them to hold it instead in working memory (Sweller et al., 2020). I have thought about that a lot in my work, and have concluded that the words, phrases, and sentences generated by students in my classes should all be written with the idea of revisiting them in various ways:

- to analyse them as new information is introduced
- to alter them when new concepts are learned
- to review them in copying and dictation activities.

This recycling, if done thoughtfully, can lead to deeper, more permanent learning across any number of subjects. I recommend having a specific exercise book that students return to as the lessons unfold, rather than odd bits of paper that float away, or whiteboards that get erased. Make a Language for Life exercise book an integral part of every student's classroom library.

Finally, the scripts, illustrations, marking system, and deeper lessons on the parts of speech can be done when your students are ready. With a good grounding, like the activities suggested in the early years, it is possible that your students will be ready sooner than you think. Enjoy the journey!

Lyn Stone

Figure 0.3 Dragon illustration

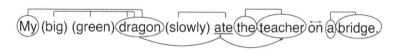

Figure 0.4 Fully marked dragon sentence

1 Nouns

Syntactic royalty

Definition

Nouns name people, places, things, feelings, or ideas.

Etymology

Latin *nomen* 'name'. This is why when you *nominate* someone, you say their *name*.

Marking

Put a circle around the nouns.

Figure 1.1 Noun instructions

Story

Nouns are the royal family of the word world. In sentences, they are the focus. They have special helpers who do all kinds of jobs, just for them.

Figure 1.2 Noun illustration

DOI: 10.4324/9781003457930-1

Teaching notes

You will need:

• laminated word cards (Appendix 3)
• nouns worksheet

Nouns are a fairly easy category to identify. The interesting and somewhat lesser-known aspect of nouns is that they have parts of speech that serve them exclusively. If you look at the parts of speech diagram (Fig 0.1), you'll see that the noun section has two other lexical categories (determiners and pronouns) within it. They have specific noun-related functions.

Adverbs and conjunctions interact with the other word categories, but adjectives and prepositions are in the exclusive servitude of nouns, and will always be connected to a noun. This is why nouns get the label 'syntactic royalty' in this analysis.

In full sentences, nouns also interact with verbs, of course, but verbs have equal status in that they are required if a grammatical utterance is to take place.

Compound nouns

Some nouns comprise two words (club sandwich, soda pop, Loch Ness). Multiple words functioning as one lexical unit can be confusing. It happens with verbs too, as we will soon see (*will see* in this sentence constituted one verb).

This process of recombination of words to form new concepts is a common device in language. It saves us having to invent completely new words all the time. German is particularly adept at this and actually goes as far as often leaving no spaces between words when new words are formed. The wonderful *Rindfleischetikettierungsüberwachungsaufgabenübertragungsgesetz*, meaning 'the law concerning the delegation of duties for the supervision of cattle marking and the labelling of beef', has now been de-commissioned, since the Mad Cow no longer troubles the German government. It demonstrates the point quite well, though.

In English, compound nouns often begin as two separate nouns (*trick shot*). Sometimes, they start to lean towards each other by virtue of a hyphen (*trick-shot*) and indeed, if their adjacent borders are friendly to one another in sound and/or meaning, they often become one word (*trickshot* but not so much *dogs-expo*).

Some sequences of words have a different meaning when brought together than when they are apart (*apart* is an example). This can cause confusion in some quarters and outrage in others. Take the words *every* and *day*. When they are adjacent in a sentence they mean 'on all days', but when together they mean 'ordinary'. Does anyone else feel a pang of righteous pique when they see signs like 'Breakfast served everyday'? Really? What do I have to do to get a special breakfast around here?[1]

This happens quite frequently these days, with words like *every* and *any*, and is a change that threatens to offend many, but change will continue nevertheless. Or is it never the less?

Compounds are used throughout the lessons and are treated as one word.

When nouns look like verbs

It can sometimes get confusing when nouns end in suffixes traditionally associated with verbs (i.e. -ing). For example:

Eating is his favourite pastime.

The subject of this sentence is 'eating'. It could be replaced with 'origami' or 'judo'. Just because it ends with -ing doesn't make it a verb. That's why studying parts of speech in isolation will never work well. You have to take into account the word's behaviour and relationships in context.

Nouns worksheet solution and notes

Definition

A noun is a word that names a person, place, thing, feeling, or idea.
    Noun examples:

Person: *Chloe, Sasha, Imogen, Mrs Chips*
Place: *Motherwell, Moonee Ponds, Toronto*

---

1 Please see Chapter 22, the 'Language change' chapter, for an apology about my little outburst there.

Thing: *bear, coffee, keys*
Feeling: *happiness, envy, joy*
Idea: *love, peace, harmony*

Example passage: The example passage should look like this, with each noun circled:

Ravens are very intelligent birds. They often use tools, such as sticks and other objects, to extract insects from tight spaces.

Figure 1.3 Noun example passage marked

Student sentences

The self-generated sentences on this first worksheet will be returned to in future lessons, so please ensure they are neat, grammatical, and easily found again.

Activities

Activity 1.1 – Pointing

To introduce the concept of concrete, as opposed to abstract nouns, have students partner up and look around the room. Each student points to five things, telling their partner what these things are.

Tell students that the part of speech they are using is a noun.

Activity 1.2 – Heartfelt

To introduce the concept of abstract nouns, point to your heart and say, 'The thing that I'm feeling in my heart today is happiness.'

Ask students point to their hearts in turn and complete the sentence 'The thing that I'm feeling in my heart today is . . .'

Tell students that the part of speech they are using is an abstract noun.

Watch out!

Students will try to squeeze adjectives in here, as it almost makes sense to say, 'The thing that I'm feeling in my heart today is happy.'

Handle this by saying,

You've got the right base there, but let's see if *happy* really does the same job as the other nouns we mentioned. We can do this by testing the words in a sentence.

Let's take a noun we're comfortable with, like *dragon*. Does the sentence *My dragon ate the teacher* make sense? (YES)

Let's replace the noun *dragon* with this word *happy*. What is the sentence now? (MY HAPPY ATE THE TEACHER)

Does this make sense? (NO)

Happy is not a thing, *happy* describes a thing, making it an adjective, which we'll deal with later. To turn the word *happy* into a noun, we have to add at the suffix -ness at the end. It also undergoes a spelling change, where the <y> becomes an <i>. This happens in other adjective to noun conversions, like *silliness*, *spiciness*, and *heaviness*.

We will do some more noun tests shortly.

Activity 1.3 – Test sentences

For parts of speech like nouns, verbs, and adjectives, you can do some fairly simple tests to confirm their lexical category. Context, however, is always the best adjudicator when it comes to parts of speech.

Gather up your laminated word cards from Appendix 3 and display them in random order.

Write the three test sentences where they can be seen, and place each word in each of the three sentences, one by one. You will find that any noun will make sense in at least one of the sentences while none of the other words will.

Watch out!

Words can be homonyms, i.e. they can have two separate meanings but the same letter sequence. An example is *run*, as in *We run* (verb) and *We are ready for the run* (noun).

If your students point this out, they are to be congratulated for their observation. At this stage, though, if *run* does come up as being ambiguous, ask your students to wait until later in the program before a full explanation is revealed.

The three test sentences are as follows:

1 This is the _____.
2 (The) _____ seems fine.
3 The teacher's _____ is okay.

Important note: when using test sentence 2, always use the word *the* at the beginning unless you are testing a proper noun, otherwise, pronouns will also fit.

Test sentence suggested dialogue

I have fifteen example words here. By the time we finish this course, we will have worked out together exactly what jobs these words do and how they can be connected to each other in sentences. Knowing this will help you be a stronger reader and writer.

Let's go through the words now and see if they make sense in these sentences. If they don't, then we can be pretty sure they're not nouns. This is a good test for later on, when you are looking at all the parts of speech together.

Take the word cards and put each word in the three test sentences. If a word makes sense in at least one sentence, move it to the right of the board. If the word doesn't make sense in any sentence, move it to the left.

You should end up with three words on the right (*James*, *cat*, and *idea*) and twelve words on the left.

Activity 1.4 – Noun classes

Nouns can be put into groups on the basis of what they name. Here are some common groups.

Proper nouns

These are the specific names for people, places, and things. They always start with a capital letter:

- names of people: Johnny, Stephen, Cecily
- names of places: Loch Lomond, Lake Eyre, Lake Victoria
- names of days and months: Friday, Christmas Eve, March
- titles of books, films, and shows: Burmese Days, Ordinary People, Friends, Cats
- brand names: Microsoft, Universal Pictures, Firefox, Apple

Note: We also capitalise the following kinds of words:

- the first word of a sentence, even if it's not a noun
- the word *I*

Q. Why do you think we do this?

In German, all nouns are capitalised. A few centuries ago we also used to do this in English, but this practice fell away and now only words deemed significant, such as sentence beginnings and names, are capitalised.

Worksheet: Guide students to write some proper nouns of their own.

Common nouns

These are used to name things within a general group but are not the specific *name* of these things. For example, *country* names a type of place generally and is a common noun. *India* names a specific place in the group *country* and is a proper noun.

If we were to use personification again, proper nouns are the names we would use if we were sitting around a dinner table with friends or family. We wouldn't say, 'Girl, pass me the salt please.' Instead, we would use her name:

'Holly, pass me the salt please.' Similarly if books had families, they wouldn't simply address one another as 'book'. Instead they would say things like, 'Hey, *To Kill a Mockingbird*, pass me the salt please.'

In the worksheet: Guide students to write some common nouns of their own and to compare those to proper nouns.

Countable nouns

These nouns are a subset of common nouns. As the name suggests, they name something that can be counted and therefore can take a singular or a plural form. Some examples are *birds*, *ravens*, *trees*, and *nests*.

Mass nouns

In contrast with countable nouns, mass nouns name things that cannot be counted, such as *justice* or *freedom*.

Worksheet: Guide students to write some mass nouns and compare them to countable nouns.

Abstract nouns

When we talked about what we were feeling in our hearts, we were using abstract nouns. These are things you can't see, and include feelings, thoughts, and ideas.

Worksheet: Guide students to write some abstract nouns of their own.

Collective nouns

These name groups of related things. Most of the collective nouns in English name groups of animals, but some also apply to people:

- a *parliament* of owls
- a *mob* of kangaroos
- a *conspiracy* of lemurs
- a *bevy* of beauties.

Nouns worksheet

Put a circle around the nouns.

1 Circle the nouns in the example sentence.

My big green dragon slowly ate the teacher on a bridge.

2 Write the definition.

A noun is

_____

_____

3 Write some examples of common nouns and proper nouns.

Common nouns

_____   _____   _____

Proper nouns

people   _____   _____   _____

places   _____   _____   _____

titles   _____   _____   _____

Lyn Stone (2025), *Language for Life* (2nd Ed.), Routledge

4 Fill in the blanks in the table below to match the first example.

Table 1.1 Common vs proper nouns

Common noun	Proper noun
planet	Jupiter
country	
	Hogwarts
car	
	Kermit

5 Write some examples of the following types of nouns.

Countable nouns

_____   _____   _____

Mass nouns

_____   _____   _____

Abstract nouns

feelings   _____   _____   _____

ideas   _____   _____   _____

Collective nouns

_____

_____

_____

6 Use three of your nouns in sentences and circle them.

a _____

b _____

c _____

Lyn Stone (2025), *Language for Life* (2nd Ed.), Routledge

Ravens are very intelligent birds.

They often use tools, such as

sticks and other objects, to extract

insects from tight spaces.

Lyn Stone (2025), *Language for Life* (2nd Ed.), Routledge

2 Determiners

Noun heralds

Definition

A word class that precedes adjectives and limits a noun. The definite and indefinite articles (*a* and *the*) are the most commonly recognised determiners. Articles, however, are a subset of the larger class *determiners*.

Because nouns are syntactic royalty, determiners, in this analysis, are called *noun heralds*. A herald does the job of announcing the approach of something important ('Hark! The herald angels sing'). Determiners announce the arrival of a noun.

Etymology

de + termine ('end, limit') + er → determiner

Marking

Determiners in our example sentences will also be circled, since their relationship to nouns is so close. They will be connected to their nouns with a superscript line.

Put a circle around the determiners and connect them to their nouns with a superscript line.

Figure 2.1 Determiner instructions

DOI: 10.4324/9781003457930-2

Figure 2.2 Determiner illustration

Story

Determiners are noun-servants whose job it is to carry important information about the noun coming along. In the old days, a servant who did this kind of job was called a herald.

Teaching notes

Though somewhat descriptive, and, in some approaches, lumped in with adjectives, determiners are distinct from adjectives like *big* or *green* in that they limit their noun by telling us whether it is:

- singular or plural (*this/these*)
- definite or indefinite (*the/a*)
- belonging to someone or something (*my, your, their*).

Further, determiners can be placed into certain categories, including:

- articles (*the, a, an*)
- demonstratives (*this, that, these*)
- quantifiers (*one, more, many*)
- possessives (*my, your, their*).

There is much scope for argument regarding determiners. Some would call them pronouns; some would call them adjectives. Some say they are not a word class at all but are structural rather than functional words.

Which arguments are acceptable to you is a personal decision. This lesson is an indication of where I sit on the subject, but hearing arguments about it is both welcome and pleasing.

What we can agree on about determiners is that they usually come before adjectives in grammatical sentences:

The black raven caught an insect.
*Black the raven caught an insect.

Also, certain nouns don't need determiners at all. These are:

- Nouns referring to generic things:

  Biologists enjoy life.

- Nouns referring to a single group of things:

  Ravens hunt insects, which has a different sense from *Ravens hunt the insects.*

- Proper nouns:

  Tony shucked the oysters, not **the Tony shucked the oysters*. Putting articles before proper nouns denotes a special kind of egotism: *The Todd is happy*.

Here is a list of some common determiners. Go back through the nouns your students wrote in the previous lesson and place some determiners before those nouns. See how they change.

ARTICLES	DEMONSTRATIVES
the	this
a	that
an	these

QUANTIFIERS	POSSESSIVES
one	my
more	your
many	their

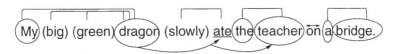

Figure 2.3 Determiner dragon sentence marked

Activities

Activity 2.1 – Determiners in the example sentence

Review the example sentence *My big green dragon slowly ate the teacher on a bridge*. Discuss the role of *my*, *the*, and *a*. The ideas you are looking for are that they refer to the nouns being singular or plural, definite or indefinite, belonging to someone or something, etc.

As you can see, the word *my* is separated from its noun by the two words *big* and *green*. They also tell us more about the noun, but in a way that describes the noun. We will look more closely at this a little later. In the dragon sentence, the word *my* is called the *dragon*'s determiner. Draw a line from *my* to *dragon*, jumping over the two words *big* and *green*. This shows how the determiner is connected to the noun.

Determiners are special type of noun-servant; they announce that a noun is coming and they say a little bit about the noun's role in the sentence.

When a determiner and a noun are combined, we have what's called a **noun phrase**. We will do more work on phrases later on.

Activity 2.2 – Example passage

Have students go to their own previously written sentences and circle any determiners, connecting them to their nouns. The example passage will look like this:

Figure 2.4 Determiner example passage marked

Worksheet

1. Go to your sentences and circle and connect your determiners and nouns.
2. Mark the dragon sentence.
3. Mark the example passage.

Put a circle around the determiners and connect them to their nouns with a superscript line.

The Australian raven is a large bird.

Lyn Stone (2025), *Language for Life* (2nd Ed.), Routledge

3 Pronouns
Syntactic stunt doubles

Definition

Pronouns are words that make us think of nouns. They stand in for nouns and usually have a noun preceding them, called a 'referent'.

Etymology

pro- 'in place of' + *nomen* 'name' pronoun

Marking

Pronouns in our example sentences will also be circled, since their relationship to nouns and determiners is so close.

Story

Pronouns are the stunt-doubles of sentences, jumping in for nouns whenever they are needed. Their work as stand-ins helps to keep sentences from being too repetitive.

Figure 3.1 Pronoun illustration

DOI: 10.4324/9781003457930-3

Teaching notes

You will need:

- Pronouns worksheet
- Laminated word cards (Appendix 3)
- Pronouns example passage

In this analysis, pronouns are called the 'syntactic stunt doubles' because in sentences, they are the stand-ins for nouns and noun phrases. Like much of human behaviour, language bends towards economy and pronouns help us economise. They are relatively small function words, standing in for longer content words. They are easier to say and so they are easier to write. This helps us communicate more fluently. Hooray for pronouns!

Function and content words

The words we use in English can be split into two rough groups: function words and content words.

Function words are those that we use to express grammatical relationships between words and phrases. These are typically determiners, pronouns, prepositions, and conjunctions. Without the content words around them, they are hard to define. Content words are the major contributors to the meaning of sentences; the nouns, verbs, adjectives, and adverbs. They can be clearly defined, independent of sentences.

The interesting thing about function words is that they are pretty much a closed class of words, that is, we are not making up many new function words. That's not the case for content words. For example, in the very recent past, a new noun came into the vocabulary of most people on Earth. The noun was Covid. We're making up new nouns, verbs, adjectives, and adverbs all the time. We're not, however, making up new determiners, pronouns, prepositions, or conjunctions in quite the same way.

How to study pronouns

Pronouns are not particularly complex, and, in my view, need not be over-taught in the classroom, otherwise the lessons begin to resemble an English as an additional language class. Children typically understand pronouns as a natural function of oral language development.

The useful part of pronoun study is to help identify and correct *pronoun switching* using some simple metalanguage. An example of *pronoun switching*:

The brolga is a large water bird. They live in Australia. (The subject of first sentence was singular noun but the following pronoun indicated a plural noun. The sentence should have read: *The brolga is a large water bird. It lives in Australia./Brolgas are large water birds. They live in Australia.*)

We will begin with some simple pronoun identification exercises.

Next, we are going to do some exercises replacing pronouns with nouns to get a sense of their function. This then sets us up to offer feedback when pronoun switching occurs.

Pronouns can be further divided into classes depending on their function in sentences. Table 3.1 lists the English pronouns and indicates what class they belong to.

Pronouns example passage

Please note that this is the first example of words being connected to one another while they occupy different lines. This will happen more and more, and with other parts of speech, as the lessons progress. Don't forget to explicitly instruct your students to make a black dot at the end of the line and one at the beginning of the next line to anchor the line across these breaks.

Table 3.1 Pronouns

Class	Pronoun
Personal	I, me, you, he, him, she, her, it, we, you, they, them
Possessive	my, mine, your, yours, his, hers, her, its, our, ours, their, theirs
Reflexive	myself, yourself, himself, herself, itself, ourselves, yourselves, themselves
Relative	who, whom,[1] which, that
Interrogative	who, whom, what, which, whose
Demonstrative	this, these, that, those
Indefinite	anyone, anybody, someone, somebody, everyone, everybody, no one, nobody

1 *whom:* This word is still very much in use in formal language, but is almost obsolete in informal speech. It is good to understand it, but its use is no longer mandatory.

Figure 3.2 Pronoun example passage marked

Activities

Activity 3.1 – Replacement

Previously we looked at words that name things. What part of speech were they? (NOUNS)

In this lesson, we're going to look at words that stand for or make us think of nouns. They are still included in the noun space because of this.

They are called pronouns, and like stunt actors in movies, they go in place of nouns to stop us having to repeat the same word over and over. Some nouns are big and complicated, so having pronouns in their place helps us to communicate faster and with less energy.

Look at the words in the dragon sentence and tell me if there are any words that you could replace with a noun. (*MY* COULD BE REPLACED WITH SOMEONE'S NAME)

Underneath the word *my*, write your name. You'd have to change your name a bit to make the sentence make sense though. How would you change it? (BY ADDING THE SUFFIX -'*S*)

When you change a word like this so that it agrees with the other parts of the sentence, that's called changing a word's *form*. We do that automatically in speech from the time we're very young.

The word *my* stands in for a noun. Therefore, it is a pronoun. Let's write the definition on the worksheet.

Definition: A pronoun is a word that stands for a noun.

Activity 3.2 – Marking

We're going to mark pronouns in sentences in the same way that we mark nouns and determiners. How do we do this? (BY CIRCLING THEM)

Why are we marking them the same as nouns? (BECAUSE PRONOUNS STAND FOR NOUNS)

Look carefully at the words in the example passage on the worksheet. The paragraph is about a type of bird called a *brolga*. The passage doesn't continue to use the word *brolga*, but instead you can see words that make us think of brolgas or of the person reading the paragraph. What words? (IT, YOU, THEM)

Words that make us think of nouns in this way are called pronouns. Now circle all the nouns, determiners, and pronouns in the passage.

Activity 3.3 – A world without pronouns

Here is another activity we can do to demonstrate pronouns.

Imagine a world with no pronouns. In our example passage, every time the brolga or another noun is mentioned, they would have to be written in full. For example, take the second sentence: *It is also known as the Australian crane.*

How would we say that sentence without pronouns? (THE BROLGA IS ALSO KNOWN AS THE AUSTRALIAN CRANE)

Now let's write out the whole paragraph, taking out the pronouns and putting the nouns they are referring to. How does it read now?

The brolga is a large waterbird. The brolga is also known as the Australian crane. The brolga is found primarily in wetlands and grasslands, but the reader can also find brolgas in open forests and farms.

That's a lot of brolgas, and how awkward does it sound when the paragraph refers to the reader. We don't write or speak like that at all!

Activity 3.4 – Student sentences without pronouns

Have students revisit the sentences they wrote for the noun lesson. This time have them write the sentences again using pronouns in place of the nouns. Have them circle the pronouns in their sentences.

Activity 3.5 – Test sentences

Write the four test sentences below.

1 He is washing a dog.
2 I saw the horses.
3 They went out.
4 It is bright red.

Place your laminated noun cards on the board.

In the first sentence, *He is washing a dog*, can anyone tell me if I could take out a word and replace it with a word on one of the noun cards? (YES, YOU COULD REPLACE *HE* WITH *JAMES* AND YOU COULD RE-PLACE *DOG* WITH *CAT*)

That's right, you could swap one noun for another, such as *cat* for *dog*, or you could take out the word *he* and put someone's name there, because the word *he* is meant to make you think of someone. What kind of word makes you think of a noun? (A PRONOUN)

From now on, whenever we find a word that can stand in for or replace any type of noun, we're going to call it a pronoun.

Repeat this process with the other noun cards and the remaining test sentences.

Pronouns worksheet

1 Write the definition of a pronoun.

_____

_____

2 Circle the nouns and their determiners and the pronouns in the following
   passage.

The brolga is a large waterbird. It is

also known as the Australian

crane. It is found primarily in

wetlands and grasslands, but you

can also find it in open forests and

farms.

Lyn Stone (2025), *Language for Life* (2nd Ed.), Routledge

3 Rewrite the passage, replacing all the pronouns with nouns.

_____

_____

_____

_____

_____

4 Rewrite your sentences from the nouns lesson, this time using pronouns in place of any nouns.

a _____

b _____

c _____

Lyn Stone (2025), *Language for Life* (2nd Ed.), Routledge

Extension activities

These extension activities are for students wishing to do further work on pronouns. There are several different types of pronoun. The list below identifies the major categories. The list gives each pronoun a name and a function and some examples. Extension students can use this list to determine what kinds of pronouns appear in the example passages from now on.

Personal pronouns

These refer to:

- the speaker(s): *I, me, we, us*
- the person or people being spoken to: *you*
- or the person/people being spoken about: *he, him, she, her, it, they, them.*

Note: *you* was originally the second person plural. The singular was *thou/ thee*. *Thou/thee* is still sometimes used in some dialects of English but is rapidly disappearing. Some English dialects change the form of the second person plural to *youse*. This happens in many versions of English spoken in parts of Australia, Scotland, Ireland, the USA, and England. Another American version of this is *y'all*.

Discuss the different uses of personal pronouns and the kinds of sentences they appear in.

Possessive pronouns

These pronouns match the personal pronouns and stand in for a noun or noun phrase (we will come to phrases shortly):

my, mine, your, yours, his, hers, her, its, our, ours, their, theirs

Note: There is no apostrophe at the end of any of the possessive pronouns. This helps to remind us of the difference between *its*, as in:

Its blanket was soaked.

and the contraction *it's*, as in:

It's a nice day.

Why do you think people have problems differentiating between the two?

Reflexive pronouns

These are the personal pronouns plus the suffix *-self* or *-selves*:

   myself, yourself, himself, herself, itself, ourselves, yourselves, themselves

Sometimes people use reflexive pronouns in a non-standard way to try to appear more formal, polite or courteous. *And for yourself, Madam?* or *Please forward the document to myself*. Other languages do have alternative, more formal pronouns (French: *tu/vous*, German: *du/Sie*), but usually for second person pronouns only.

   More information about this can be found in the Language Myths chapter.

Relative pronouns worksheet

These include:

who, whom, which, that

These pronouns show the connection between a noun and the rest of the sentence.

The word *that* can also be used in this way and people often interchange it with *which*. However, there can be a difference. Consider the meaning of the sentences below.

The pig, *which* is black, slept soundly in the sty.
The pig *that* is black slept soundly in the sty.

The first sentence implies that there is only one pig and that, incidentally, it is black, whereas the second sentence implies that there is more than one pig, but only the black one slept soundly in the sty. The commas are also helpful here.

Create some more sentences where *which* and *that* imply this subtle difference.

_____

_____

_____

Lyn Stone (2025), *Language for Life* (2nd Ed.), Routledge

Interrogative pronouns worksheet

inter + roge ('request') + ate + ive → interrogative

These pronouns are often referred to as question words (to *interrogate* is to question someone):

who, whom, what, which, whose

We have seen some of these words categorised as relative pronouns above, but the way in which they are used differs. While relative pronouns simply show relationship, interrogative pronouns are used to form questions.

They can also introduce another part of a sentence to form a different kind of question:

Andy wondered *who* played the solo.
Joanna is trying to find out *whose* mess this is.
Caitlin asked Ory *what* he said.

Write some more examples of interrogative pronouns forming the introduction to the second part of the sentence.

_____

_____

_____

Lyn Stone (2025), *Language for Life* (2nd Ed.), Routledge

Demonstrative pronouns

These interesting words take singular or plural form depending on the follow-ing noun:

These *this/these*: this town/these things
that/those: that mistake/those shoes

'Demonstrative pronouns could also fall into the determiners category since they signal a noun.' Discuss.

Indefinite pronouns worksheet

These pronouns do not make particular reference to an identifiable person or thing.

These, all, any, each, every, none, no, one, some

Use each one in an example sentence to see how this might be true.

_____
_____
_____
_____
_____
_____
_____
_____
_____
_____
_____
_____
_____
_____
_____
_____
_____
_____
_____
_____
_____
_____
_____
_____
_____
_____
_____
_____
_____

Lyn Stone (2025), *Language for Life* (2nd Ed.), Routledge

Reciprocal pronouns

These pronouns show mutual action and are limited to:

these, each other, one another

Are they interchangeable or do they differ slightly in meaning?

Compound pronouns

These pronouns are formed using the indefinite pronouns *any, every, no*, and *some*, plus the endings *-body, -one, -thing, -where*.

anybody, anyone, anything, anywhere, everybody, everyone, everything, everywhere, nobody, no one, nothing, nowhere, somebody, someone, something, somewhere

In some dialects, the ending *-how* is also acceptable, but is not generally recognised as a standard form of English, except the word *somehow*:

anyhow, nohow

Which do you find more acceptable and why do you think *every* is missing from this list?

His/her/their

The pronouns *he* and *she* are gender specific. What happens when the subject doesn't reveal the gender? Consider:

A person could break his/her neck on that step.

Which pronoun do you choose?

A person could break his neck on that step.
A person could break her neck on that step.

Some writers choose *their*, though this is considered less formal, some choose one gender and stick with it in whatever they are writing, and others alternate between the genders.

What's your preference?

4 Verbs

The movers and shakers

When I have previously taught verbs I have fallen into the trap of defining them as *action words* with my students. Your explanation of them has made me better understand verbs. Thanks!

Primary school teacher after completing
Language for Life Online

Definition

Verbs are words that express actions, states of being, and states of having.

Etymology

Latin *verbum* 'word', possibly from Sanskrit *vrata* 'command, vow'

Marking

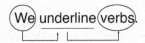

Figure 4.1 Verb instructions

When diagramming sentences, we circle nouns and place a line underneath verbs. We show their relationship with a subscript arrow. Fig 4.2 illustrates this relationship, the criteria for categorising words as verbs, and the minimal components of a grammatical sentence.

DOI: 10.4324/9781003457930-4

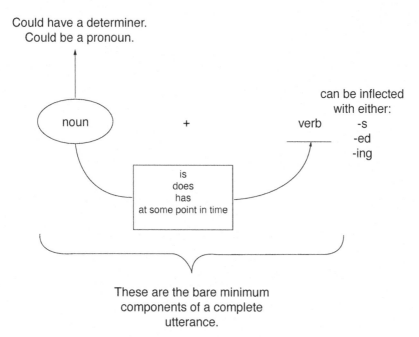

Figure 4.2 Minimal sentence components

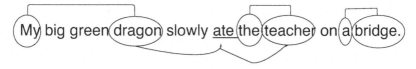

Figure 4.3 Verb dragon sentence marked

Story

If nouns are the royal family, then verbs are the governors, carrying out the commands of the ruling classes. Verbs show what the nouns are doing, being, and having and even show when those noun experiences are taking place. This teamwork makes sentences come alive.

Figure 4.4 Verb illustration

Teaching notes

When searching for a list of verb types, it is not hard to get the feeling that the list might never end. The lessons in this chapter, however, will be limited to a study of:

- transitive verbs
- intransitive verbs
- auxiliary verbs
- modal verbs

Tense and agreement, also vital aspects of verb study, will be dealt with in subsequent chapters.

The Verb Test

To test whether a word in a sentence is a verb or is not a verb we can use the Verb Test.

If one or all of the below is true, then you have a verb:

1 If X is a verb, you can put it into the past tense by adding the suffix -ed (this isn't done with irregular verbs, hence the label 'irregular'), e.g. *helped*, *walked* but not *ran*.
2 If X is a verb, you can add the suffix -s in the third person singular, e.g. *helps*, *walks*, *runs*.
3 If X is a verb, you can put it into the continuous tense by adding the suffix -ing, e.g. *helping*, *walking*, *running*. Even the supremely irregular verb *be* can be inflected this way. -ing is one fabulous suffix!

In earlier works, I have referred to verbs as simply *be, do, have* words, but have now expanded my definition to encompass verbs that link their subjects and objects in something other than a being, doing, or having way.

Take, for example, the verb *appreciate* in the sentence:

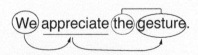

Figure 4.5 Verb expressing experience

The subject, *we*, is linked to the object *gesture* through the verb, *appreciate.* We are not strictly doing, being, or having anything, but instead are referring to the experience of a feeling.

Auxiliary verbs

Sometimes the whole verb in a sentence comprises several words, consisting of a main verb and what is called an auxiliary verb/verbs. There is a small set of auxiliary verbs, which we call a closed set. The set of possible main verbs in our language is endless, as you can keep on inventing new words for all our experiences, e.g. *pixelate, unfriend*, etc. This type of set is called an open set. The words *is* and *running* in the sentence below are examples of an auxiliary verb and a main verb.

Figure 4.6 Auxiliary verb example

If we allow verbs about experience, such as *appreciate* above, to be a subset of doing verbs, an interesting pattern occurs. We can classify all verbs under the banner of 'be, do, have' words:

being: *am, is, look, smell, appear, seem*
doing: *surf, dive, ski*
having: *have, possess, own*

The words *be, do, have*, and their various forms also comprise a set of words known as 'auxiliary verbs' which in turn help us express the time of the be/do/have or other nuances such as habitual action, general truths, emphasis, or even negation. We will study the way they compound with main verbs to deliver very precise information about their nouns.

Modal verbs

Slightly different from auxiliary verbs are modal verbs. These also deliver precise information about their nouns and their main verbs. There is an overlap between modal verbs and what we sometimes call future tense, as we will soon see.

The major modal verbs in English are:

can, could, may, might, must, shall, should, will, would

Their job is to alter the main verb by expressing certain 'moods', if you like. Those moods are:

ability, certainty, desire, obligation, permission

Ability: This fish can live in this water.
Certainty (low): This fish might live in this water.
Certainty (high): This fish should live in this water.
Certainty (absolute): This fish will live in this water.
Desire: This fish would like to live in this water.
Obligation: You should put that fish in this water.
Permission: You may put that fish in this water.

Implied subjects

Complete thoughts can be communicated without mentioning a noun or pronoun. Consider these examples:

Stop the bus.
Take that back!
Duck!

Each time, the subject implied is *you*, the person being spoken to. Sentences, known as imperatives, where the speaker is directing or commanding the listener, often have implied subjects. More on that in the phrases, clauses, and sentences chapters.

Subject–verb–object

Nouns can also be connected to verbs by being a receiving point. When a verb affects a noun in this way, that noun is its object. One of my linguistics tutors likened it to the energy transferred through the action of a billiard ball. The stick hits the ball, which then goes on to hit another ball. The marking

Figure 4.7 Subject–verb–object diagram

in Figure 4.7 serves to illustrate the transfer of energy from the subject, through the verb to the object.

Transitive and intransitive verbs

in + trans ('across') + ite ('go') + ive → intransitive

The diagram below illustrates the components of a simple sentence where there is one subject and one verb, such as:

Birds fly.

If we were to carry on the transfer of energy from *birds* through *fly* and wanted to name an object that birds flew, we could say something like:

Birds fly helicopters.

Now we have a subject–verb–object construction and the difference between intransitive and transitive verbs:
Many verbs can be both transitive and intransitive. For example:

The dog is *running.*
The dog is *running* the country.

In the first sentence, the dog is doing the action of going fast on its legs. In the second sentence, the dog is doing something connected with the governing of a country. The verb in the first sentence is intransitive and the verb in the second is transitive.

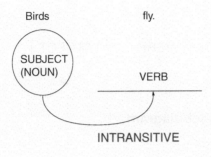

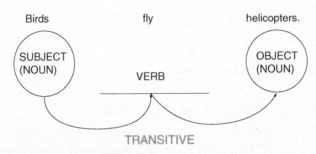

Figure 4.8 Transitive/intransitive verbs

The verbs listed below are some examples of intransitive verbs. Some of them can be used transitively as well. That is, some can take an object in certain contexts. For instance, *escape* in *We will escape* is intransitive, but in *I escaped his attention* the verb is now transitive, *his attention* being the object of the verb *escape*.

act, adapt, admit, answer, attack, bat, be, bite, camp, cheat, clash, crawl, dabble, dance, detract, do, elope, emigrate, erupt, escape, expand, explode, fade, fall, fast, fidget, flit, float, fly, frolic, gallop, glow, grow, jump, kneel, lead, lean, leap, learn, left, limp, listen, march, mourn, move, panic, party, pause, peep, pose, pounce, pout, pray, preen, read, recline, relax, relent, rise, roll, run, rush, sail, scream, shake, shout, sigh, sit, skip, slide, smell, snarl, soak, spin, spit, sprint, squeak, stagger, stand, swim, swing, twist, wade, walk, wander, wave, whirl, wiggle, work, yell

Verbs worksheet notes

Sentence solutions:

Figure 4.9 Verb worksheet 1c 1d solution

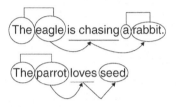

Figure 4.10 Verb worksheet 3a 3b solution

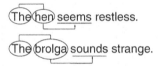

Figure 4.11 Verb worksheet 4a 4b solution

Figure 4.12 Verb worksheet 5a 5b solution

The scrambled sentences read like this:

Verbs have a subject, which is a noun or pronoun. They can also have an object, which is also a noun or pronoun.

Verbs also show state of being.

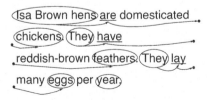

Figure 4.13 Verb example passage solution

Activities

Activity 4.1 – The Verb Test

Aside from just defining verbs, we can do a test with our verb cards to see if the words we are dealing with are verbs. They have to be able to make sense, in one of the following sentences:

1 Today I ___, yesterday I ___ed.
2 He ___s in the evening.
3 We were ___ing all day.
4 We were ___ing that yesterday.

Activity 4.2 – Complete my thought

We know what parts of speech name things or make us think of names of things. What are they called? (NOUNS AND PRONOUNS)

But when we communicate, we also need to talk about other things. We don't live in a world where we just go around naming things.

For example, tell me what's wrong with my communication if I just say this:

The dog.

Is that a complete thought? (NO)

Why not? (THERE ISN'T ENOUGH INFORMATION)

How would you make *The dog* into a complete thought? (BY TALKING ABOUT WHAT THE DOG IS DOING/EXPERIENCING, WHAT THE DOG IS LIKE OR WHAT THE DOG HAS)

Let's see if we can complete the thought by talking about what the dog is doing.

Have the students come up with ideas and then use the following example:

The dog is running.

We've added some words in order to complete our thought. We now know not only that there is a dog, but also what it is doing. What word or words show what it is doing? (IS RUNNING)

Those words are doing a different job from the nouns and pronouns. What are they doing? (THEY ARE SHOWING THE ACTION OF THE DOG)

A word that shows action is called a verb.

A simple way to show how the noun and the verb relate to each other is to use an arrow. Is the dog doing the running? (YES)

If the noun is doing the action, this is called the subject of the sentence. We show how the subject is connected to the verb by drawing an arrow from the noun to the verb.

Go back to your dragon sentence and your other sentences and put lines under the verbs. connect them to their subjects by drawing an arrow that runs under the words (subscript).

Now let's go to 1c and 1d on your worksheet and do the same with the sentences 'The eagle is soaring' and 'The parrot was screeching'.

Activity 4.3 – Subject–verb–object

We often have sentences with two nouns or pronouns; one that is acting and one that is receiving the action. Here is an example:

The dog ate the bone.

Let's mark the nouns and underline the verb.

What is the subject of the sentence? (THE DOG)

What did the dog be, do, or have? (IT WAS EATING, A DOING VERB)

Draw an arrow from *dog* to *ate* under the words to connect them.

But there is another noun here. What is it? (BONE)

How is it connected to the dog and the action of eating? (THE BONE IS BEING EATEN BY THE DOG)

When a word is affected by the verb in this way, it is called the object of the sentence. To mark the object of the sentence, we draw an arrow from the verb to the object noun or pronoun. The arrow starts off where the subject arrow ends, thus showing us that the subject is also connected to the object. It's a bit like a transfer of energy from one noun to the next through the verb.

Activity 4.4 – State of being

Now let's look at this dog again. See what you can tell me about the verb in this sentence:

The dog feels happy.

What is the noun? (THE DOG)
    Is this sentence a complete thought? (YES)
    So what word is the verb? (FEELS)

Watch out!

Often, you will get the response *feels happy*. Correct this by saying:

You're half right. One of those words is the verb, but the other is actually doing the different job of giving more information about the dog. Which word? (HAPPY)
    This is a word called an *adjective*. More on that later. However, the word we're now left with is what? (FEELS)
    In this sentence, the word *feels* is a verb. But is it showing an action of the dog? (NO, THE DOG IS NOT DOING ANYTHING, IT IS *BEING* SOMETHING)
    Rather than showing an action, the verb *feels* shows what we call a state of being. That's another job that verbs do, so to complete our definition, we must now say that verbs can show action or state of being.

Activity 4.5 – Being vs doing

Here is a list of some being verbs:

is, feels, smells, sounds, tastes, looks, appears, seems

Many of these verbs have more than one meaning: a being meaning and a doing meaning. For example:

Richard smells his roses.

is very different from

Richard smells funny.

Which is the doing verb and which is the being verb? (SENTENCE 1 HAS THE DOING VERB AND SENTENCE 2 HAS THE BEING VERB)
  Take the list of being verbs above and write out some sentences showing the be/do contrast.

Activity 4.6 – Having

There is another kind of verb that neither shows an action nor a state of being. Consider this sentence:

The dog has a kennel.

What is the subject? (THE DOG)
  And the verb? (HAS)
  Does it have an object? (YES, *KENNEL*)
  Is the dog doing something? (NO)
  Is the dog being something? (NO)
  So what is the verb expressing here? (HAVING/POSSESSION)
  Let's think of some other verbs that express this idea.

A list of possible *having* verbs:

> *possess, own, retain, hold, exhibit, keep, lack* (the opposite of *have* in this sense, but still not expressing an action or state of being)

Activity 4.7 – Experience verbs

There is another kind of verb that neither shows an action, state of being nor having. Consider this sentence:

The dog likes a bones.

What is the subject? (THE DOG)
   And the verb? (LIKES)
   Does it have an object? (YES, *BONES*)
   Is the dog doing something? (NO)
   Is the dog being something? (NO)
   Does the dog have something? (NO)
   So what is the verb expressing here? (EXPERIENCE)
   Let's think of some other verbs that express this idea.

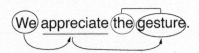

Figure 4.5 Verb expressing experience

A list of possible *experience* verbs:

> *love, appreciate, like, admire, hate, prefer, want*

Activity 4.8 – Discovering auxiliary verbs

Suggested dialogue

> In the dog sentence, there are two words that make up the verb. What two words? (IS RUNNING)
>
> There are two words there expressing the verb. *Is* and *running* go together as partners. We aren't talking about two random verbs like *eat* and *walk*, squashed together. What we have here is a main verb and an auxiliary verb. There is a small set of auxiliary verbs, which we call a closed set. The set of possible main verbs in our language is endless, as you can keep on inventing new words for all our experiences. This type of set is called an open set.
>
> We are going to mark the verb in this sentence by underlining *is running* with one line because they make up one verb.
>
> Which one do you think might be the auxiliary verb? (IS)
>
> The word *is* here certainly doesn't carry the sense of the verb. It's the word *running* that gives us the clear picture.
>
> What does *is* tell us here? (THAT THE ACTION IS TAKING PLACE IN THE PRESENT)
>
> We also need to mark the noun and its determiner.

Worksheet: There is a table of auxiliary verbs on the worksheet. Use it to discuss their role in altering the sense of a main verb.

Modal verbs

> There is another kind of verb a bit like auxiliary verbs. Consider these two sentences:
>
> *This fish can live in this water.*
> *This fish might live in this water.*

Do they mean the same thing? (NO)

What's the difference? (THE FIRST ONE IS SAYING THAT THE FISH IS ABLE TO LIVE IN THIS WATER, WHEREAS THE SECOND ONE IS SAYING THAT IT'S POSSIBLE BUT NOT CERTAIN THAT THE FISH CAN LIVE IN THIS WATER.)

I can change it again. Think about how the meaning changes:

This fish should live in this water. (HIGH CERTAINTY)

This fish will live in this water. (ABSOLUTE CERTAINTY)

This fish would like to live in this water. (DESIRE)

You should put that fish in this water. (OBLIGATION)

You may put that fish in this water. (PERMISSION)

These are called modal verbs. Their job is to alter the main verb by expressing certain 'moods', if you like.

The major modal verbs in English are:

can, could, may, might, must, shall, should, will, would

Those moods are:

ability, certainty, desire, obligation, permission

Activity 4.9 – Implied subjects

Sometimes you can communicate a complete thought without mentioning a noun or pronoun. Consider these examples:

Pass the salt. (subject *you*) *See you tomorrow.* (subject *I*)
Wish you were here. (subject *I/we*)

Such examples usually occur in less formal language.

Have your students think of some more implied subjects and reflect on the formality/informality of the utterances in which implied subjects occur.

Verbs worksheet

We underline verbs.

1a Go back to your dragon sentence and underline the verb and draw an arrow from the subject to the verb.

1b Go back to your sentences you created earlier and mark the verbs, subjects, and objects.

1c Circle the nouns/pronouns and determiners in the sentences below.

The eagle is soaring.

The parrot was screeching.

1d Now underline the verb and draw an arrow from the subject to the verb.

Auxiliary verbs

2 Take the main verb *explode* and add it to the following auxiliary verbs.

can	_____
is	_____
has	_____
may	_____
might	_____
must	_____
ought to	_____
shall	_____
should	_____
used to	_____
will	_____
would	_____

Lyn Stone (2025), *Language for Life* (2nd Ed.), Routledge

How did you have to change the form of *explode* to fit some of the auxiliary verbs?

Consider also the slightly different meanings given to *explode* as you change the auxiliary verb.

Subject–verb–object

3a Circle the nouns/pronouns and determiners in the sentences below.

The eagle is chasing a rabbit.

The parrot loves seed.

3b Now underline the verb and draw an arrow from the subject to the verb and from the verb to the object.
3c Unscramble the three sentences below. Rewrite them, cover them, and write them again. Check to see if what you wrote matches the unscrambled sentence:

can be
a noun or a pronoun.
The subject of a verb

Rewrite:

_____

_____

Cover and write again:

_____

_____

Check: Did you get it right?

also have
Verbs can
an object.

Lyn Stone (2025), *Language for Life* (2nd Ed.), Routledge

Rewrite:

_____

_____

Cover and write again:

_____

_____

Check: Did you get it right?

a noun or a pronoun.
An object
can also be

Rewrite:

_____

_____

Cover and write again:

_____

_____

Check: Did you get it right?

State of being

4a Circle the nouns/pronouns and determiners in the sentences below.

The hen seems restless.

The brolga sounds strange.

4b In the sentences below, underline the verb and draw an arrow from the subject to the verb.

Lyn Stone (2025), *Language for Life* (2nd Ed.), Routledge

4c Unscramble and rewrite this sentence:

state of being.
Verbs
also show

Rewrite:

_____

_____

Cover and write again:

_____

_____

Check: Did you get it right?

Having

5a Circle the nouns/pronouns and determiners in the sentences below.
5b Now underline the verb and draw an arrow from the subject to the verb
and from the verb to the object.

The hen has a nest.

The raven exhibits intelligence.

Implied subjects

6 What are the implied subjects in the following sentences? Discuss them
with the class.

Stop the bus.
Take that back!
Duck!

Lyn Stone (2025), *Language for Life* (2nd Ed.), Routledge

Mark the following passage:

Isa Brown hens are domesticated

chickens. They have

reddish-brown feathers. They lay

many eggs per year.

Lyn Stone (2025), *Language for Life* (2nd Ed.), Routledge

Extension activities

Intransitive verbs

As further verb study, have students read the information below, think of examples, and discuss.

> When the arrow starts at a noun and continues past the verb to another noun, the verb is called 'transitive'. When the arrow starts at a noun and stops at the verb, the verb is called 'intransitive'. This comes from the Latin in (meaning not) and trans (meaning across). The energy from the subject is not carried across to anything else by the verb.

In dictionaries, this is what is meant by *vi.* and *vt.* in the section that tells you what part of speech a word is.

State of being verbs

Q. What do many of the *being* verbs have in common?

A. They often have something to do with the senses.

5 Agreement

Teaching notes

Now that we have the essential components of a grammatical utterance, i.e. subjects and their verbs (subjects can be pronouns too!), we have to make sure that they agree with one another. This chapter gives some practice in doing just that.

Our purpose here is to establish an understanding that, when editing written work, subject–verb agreement is an important checkpoint.

When surveyed about how students could improve their written assignments, teachers invariably placed lack of subject–verb agreement high on their agendas. The focus of the lessons in this chapter will be to identify problem areas and build an understanding of how to construct sentences with a grammatically correct correspondence between verbs and their subjects.

The lessons in this chapter will clarify the following things:

- the term *agreement*
- the concept of number and person
- the process of conjugating verbs in agreement with their number and person
- common situations where subject–verb disagreement occurs
- subtle usages of group words (*team*, *congress*, *parliament*, etc.) in the hope of encouraging debate in the classroom about whether to treat them as singular or plural.

This unit will also provide extension work including compound subjects and objects.

Worksheet notes

1 The verb table should look like this:

DOI: 10.4324/9781003457930-5

Table 5.1 Conjugating the verb to be key

Number	Singular	Verb	Plural	Verb
		to be		
Person				
First: speaker	I	am	we	are
Second: spoken to	you	are	you	are
Third: spoken about	he/she/it	is	they	are

2 The sentences that need correction are below:

  a The list of items <u>are</u> on the fridge.
   The list of items <u>is</u> on the fridge.

  b The owners of the dog <u>is</u> happy.
   The owners of the dog <u>are</u> happy.

  c The books I gave my friend <u>was</u> interesting.
   The books I gave my friend <u>were</u> interesting.

  d Under the bridges <u>sail</u> a leaky boat.
   Under the bridges <u>sails</u> a leaky boat.

Activities

Activity 5.1 – Agree vs disagree

For subjects to have good relationships with their verbs, there has to be something called *agreement*. It's a bit like life. People work better together if they agree. Sentences work better if their subjects and verbs agree.

The agreement vs disagreement table below shows just how awkward sentences can sound if the subject and verb disagree.

Look at your own sentences and see if you can make the subject and the verb disagree. How awkward does it feel?

Table 5.2 Agreement vs disagreement

Agreement	Disagreement
1. A bird flies.	A bird fly.
2. A kiwi is a flightless bird.	A kiwi are a flightless bird.

Activity 5.2 – Number and person

With subject–verb agreement, there are two major features to look out for:

- number: whether the subject is singular or plural
- person: whether the subject is the speaker(s) (*I/we*), those spoken to (*you*), or those spoken about (*he, she, it, they*)

Consider sentence 1:

   A bird flies.

The subject is singular (one bird) and we are speaking *about* them. Let's break the verb *fly* into its number and person choices using a table. In grammar, this is called *conjugating* a verb.

Table 5.3 Conjugating the verb *to fly*

	to study			
Number	Singular	Verb	Plural	Verb
Person				
First: speaker	I	fly	we	fly
Second: spoken to	you	fly	you	fly
Third: spoken about	he/she/it	flies	they	fly

So when we say, 'The bird flies', we are speaking about a singular noun in the third person. That's how you say it like a grammarian. It's actually quite simple.

The third person singular verb for *fly* is *flies*. So your subject and your verb will agree if they are written in the third person singular. Any other person or number would result in the verb being *fly*, which for the third person, is ungrammatical.

*He fly.
*She fly.
*It fly.
*The bird fly.

In English, most verbs remain the same despite the number or person they refer to. It is only the third person singular that you have to watch out for.

Activity 5.3 – Conjugating the verb to be

Let's take a look at sentence 2.

The kiwi is a flightless bird.

The word *is* is the third person singular of the verb *to be*. This is an irregular verb and, as such, is conjugated differently from a regular one.

This time, we have a partially filled conjugation table. Let's fill in the rest.

Table 5.4 Conjugating the verb to be

	to be			
Number	*Singular*	*Verb*	*Plural*	*Verb*
Person				
First: speaker	I		we	
Second: spoken to	you		you	
Third: spoken about	he/she/it		they	

In the sentence 'The kiwi is a flightless bird', the subject is the singular noun, *kiwi*.

So what is the number? (SINGULAR)

And what is the person? (THIRD)

So what is the verb? (IS)

Why is there disagreement in the sentence *The kiwi are a flightless bird*? (THIRD PERSON SINGULAR NOUN WITH THIRD PERSON PLURAL VERB)

Nobody makes such obvious mistakes in writing very often, but now that you know what agreement is, we can take a look at why disagreement sometimes occurs.

Activity 5.4 – The noun closest to the verb

We most commonly make agreement mistakes when the subject is separated from the verb by other words. The further apart they are, the more difficult it can be to remember to make them agree. It makes it even harder when the word just before the verb looks like the subject but isn't.

Here is an example:

*The list of items are on the fridge.

Here, the verb is agreeing with the word just before it, plural *items*, instead of its actual subject, singular *list*. This is a common mistake. Take away the plural noun *items*, which is not the subject of the sentence, and you have:

*The list are on the fridge.

After this has been explained, students should be directed to the worksheet to circle the correct verb. They may have to perform the extra step of removing the non-subject nouns to make sure the verbs agree.

Figure 5.1 shows how marking subjects and verbs can show disagreement, even when the nearest noun differs in number from the verb.

Figure 5.1 Showing disagreement

To make the subject and the verb agree, we must change the verb so that it says:

The list of items is on the fridge.

Activity 5.5 – Group words

A subject can be singular or plural depending on the meaning of the sentence. This happens with group words like *team* and *nation*, and even the word *group* itself.

Let's look at some examples.

The word *team* means two or more people working together. When you have words that mean two or more people or things together, you have to decide whether you are talking about the people in the team, or the team itself.

For instance, if you were talking about your team in comparison with other teams you would count *team* as a singular noun, as in:

My team is the best in the league.

But if the individuals in a team were being spoken *about*, you could count *team* as a plural noun, as in:

My team are acting strangely.

It's a subtle difference. On your worksheet there are some more group words that behave like this.

Agreement worksheet

1 Conjugate the verb 'to be'.

Table 5.5 Conjugating the verb to be

Number	Singular	to be Verb	Plural	Verb
Person				
First: speaker				
Second: spoken to				
Third: spoken about				

2 Circle the subject and underline the verb in the following sentences. Check for agreement and correct any mistakes.

   a The list of items are on the fridge.
   b The bag of sweets is missing.
   c The owners of the dog is happy.
   d The books I gave my friend was interesting.
   e Wolves and my dog eat meat.
   f Under the bridges sail a leaky boat.

Some group nouns:

alliance, assembly, assortment, band, bunch, bundle, choir, club, cluster, clutch, coalition, collection, compendium, compilation, confederacy, congress, council, corpus, crew, crowd, ensemble, federation, gathering, horde, host, knot, league, line-up, mass, multitude, mob, partnership, pool, posse, set, side, squad, throng, troop, union

Lyn Stone (2025), *Language for Life* (2nd Ed.), Routledge

Extension activities

Indefinite pronouns

There are some pronouns that can make you think of more than one person but are treated like singular nouns. These are called *indefinite pronouns*. They refer to people or things without saying exactly who or what they are. For example:

> *Everybody is included.*
> **Everybody are included.*
>
> *Everything was perfect.*
> **Everything were perfect.*

When you use the pronouns *everybody* or *everything*, you don't think of an individual, but a group of people, so you should use a singular verb.

Compound subjects

When the subject of a sentence contains two or more nouns, things can get quite tricky. The general rule is: when the nouns are joined by the word *and*, they are treated as plural. Compare:

> *The raven and the kiwi were calling.*
> **The raven and the kiwi was calling.*

Here, two birds, the raven and the kiwi, function as individuals in a group, as in the *team* example above.

When the nouns are joined with words other than *and*, such as *or*, something different happens:

> *Either the raven or the kiwi was calling.*
> **Either the raven or the kiwi were calling.*

The subjects in this sentence are now treated as individuals. Either the raven was calling or the kiwi was calling. Not both.

Watch out!

When one of the nouns of the subject is singular and the other is plural, it can create a problem. Which verb would you choose here?

The chicks or the adult are/is calling.

There are good arguments for both verbs. In cases like this, though, it's best to rewrite the sentence:

Either the chicks are calling or the adult is.

Compound subject/ambiguous object

Consider the sentence:

Peter and I are going to train our dogs.

Does this mean that Peter and I jointly own some dogs or does it mean that we are each going to train a dog that we own individually?
How would you rewrite the sentence to show each proposition more clearly?

I? Me?

Which pronoun to use is sometimes very tricky when you have to choose between *I* and *me*. Consider the following dialogue:

'Who's there?'
'Me!'

There are those who would argue that the correct response is the pronoun *I*. If you tease it all out by lengthening the contraction and putting in the implied verb you would have:

'Who is there?'
'I am there.'

This view, however, is not often echoed in informal speech. It is not uncommon to hear the following:

Me and Sid drove to the seaside.

What is the more formal version of this sentence?

6 Tense

Definition

When you're speaking about an event, verbs show how two things are related:

- the time of speaking
- when the event took place.

This is the grammatical concept known as 'tense'.

Etymology

Latin *tempus* 'a portion of time'

Verb facts

Verbs show time by changing their form. Verbs are the only words in English that have this characteristic. This is called *tense*.

Switching tense in writing is a common error. This is not the same thing as expressing a different tense when appropriate. Contrast these two sentences:

> *If the kiwi finds a suitable burrow, it will build a nest.*
> **The kiwi found a burrow and builds a nest.*

It is very easy to get caught up in the sheer genius of a narrative and forget at which point on the timeline you started. This is what we are trying to avoid with these lessons.

We will introduce the concept of verbs showing tense with some simple past, present, and future exercises. We will then move on to the subtleties, such as the difference in meaning that present tense verbs can express:

- things that are happening now: *The kiwi is incubating its egg in its body.*
- things that are always true: *Kiwi produce very large eggs.*
- habitual action: *The kiwi forages for food at night.*

DOI: 10.4324/9781003457930-6

The activities in this chapter will help students understand these concepts.
Auxiliary and modal verbs help express tense, as shown in Fig 6.1:

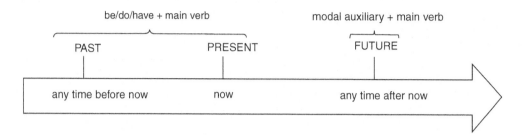

Figure 6.1 Points in time diagram

A note on irregular verbs

It has become something of a standard during our lessons to screen for and explicitly teach irregular past tense forms. We use a basic list and go through it systematically, marking correct and incorrect responses and giving around five a week to practise at home.

What this chapter will not do

Defining and naming the tenses with smaller and smaller brushstrokes is not the aim of this chapter. Separating the imperfect from the pluperfect may be useful when learning another language, but the distinction is already internalised by native speakers of English. Grasping tense does not require such exhaustive analysis.

We are merely concerned with the establishment of a common language that you and your students can share when discussing literature or when editing written work.

Activities

Activity 6.1 – Definition

Show or project the points in time diagram and discuss the three basic tenses: past, present, and future.

Activity 6.2 – Present tense and truth

The present tense shows various things. Consider the sentence:

> *The kiwi is in its nest.*

Where on the timeline would that sentence go? (IT'S HAPPENING NOW, SO IN THE 'PRESENT' SECTION)
What if I said:

> *Kiwi eat at night.*

I'm not necessarily talking about the kiwi eating right now, but I'm not talking about the past and if I was talking about the future, what would I say? (THE KIWI WILL EAT AT NIGHT)
So what do I actually mean when I use a present tense verb here? (THAT THE KIWI EATS EVERY NIGHT)
That's right. The present tense can also be used to talk about things that are always true. Here are some more examples:

> *Kiwi have marrow in their bones.*
> *Kiwi are the only birds with nostrils at the end of their beaks.*
> *Kiwi eyes are very small.*

Write a present tense sentence that shows how something is always true.

Activity 6.3 – Habitual action

Consider the statement:

> *The captive kiwi eats dog food.*

I'm using a present tense verb again but the meaning is slightly different. Unlike the constant reality of kiwi bones, nostrils, and eyes, the kiwi's diet is subject to change. It might not be true in two years when the fully grown kiwi is released into the wild. But I'm still using a present tense verb. What is this verb showing? (HABITUAL ACTION)

When we want to talk about things we do on a regular basis, we also use the present tense. Here are some more examples:

The kiwi's keepers weigh her every day.
The kiwi's enclosure is dark during the day.
Hundreds of tourists visit the kiwi every year.

Write three sentences using present tense verbs that show habitual action.

Activity 6.4 – Example sentence review

Have students look over their example sentences and determine whether any present tense verbs are showing:

a things that are happening now
b things that are always true
c habitual action.

Have students share their suggestions with the class and debate whether they are correct about what the verbs are showing.

Activity 6.5 – Past tense

Past tense verbs show things that happened in the past. We change the form of a verb to express past usually by adding the suffix *-ed*. For example:

hum   hummed
walk   walked
land   landed

A lot of our common verbs don't do this. They are called irregular verbs. *Run* is an irregular verb. When you say this word in the past tense, do you add *-ed* to *run*? (NO)
What do you say instead? (RAN)
Let's look at some more.

Brainstorm some irregular verbs – *do*, *have*, *run*, *give*, etc. – and show their past tense forms.

Have students find regular and irregular past tense verbs from their example sentences.

Activity 6.6 – Future

> You can also use verbs to express that something will be or will happen in the future. The word *will* is often used with a compound verb to show future. For example:
>
> *My cat will be three tomorrow.*
> *Our car will be fixed next week.*
> *Christmas will come early this year.*
>
> You can also use other compound verbs to show future, such as:
>
> * *is going to* + verb
> * *might* + verb
> * *shall* + verb
> * *may* + verb.
>
> Each one says a slightly different thing. Let's use each in our dragon sentence.

Substitute each compound verb and discuss the shades of meaning of each.

Worksheet

1 Write a sentence using a present tense verb that shows how something is always true:

_____

_____

2 Write a sentence using a present tense verb that shows habitual action:

_____

_____

3 Look over your example sentences and find any present tense verbs. Are they

a happening now?
b always true?
c habitual?

Lyn Stone (2025), *Language for Life* (2nd Ed.), Routledge

Parts of speech progress check

One-third of the lessons on parts of speech are now complete. Your students are familiar with subjects, verbs, and objects. Now to discover words that modify them. These are adjectives and adverbs.

The major difference between the two is that adjectives work exclusively with nouns, whereas adverbs modify verbs, adjectives, other adverbs, and whole phrases and clauses.

7   Adjectives

Descriptive noun-servants

Definition

Adjectives describe, modify, and give more information about nouns.

Etymology

Latin *ad-* 'towards' + *jacere* 'to throw' (to form *adject* 'added') – Consider the terms *subject* and *object* of a sentence. They too have this -ject element: that which is thrown into the conversation perhaps. This grammatical sense of subject and object came into literature around about 1729, according to Etymonline.

Marking

Adjectives in our example sentences will be placed in brackets with a super-script line going to the noun(s) they modify. Now our sentences are beginning to look like this:

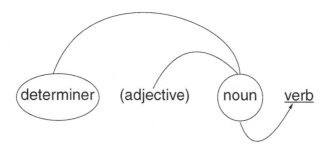

Figure 7.1 Determiner, adjective, noun, verb

DOI: 10.4324/9781003457930-7

Adjective story

The royal nouns have special helpers called adjectives. Adjectives work together with nouns to modify them. A noun can be made more interesting and colourful through the work of adjectives. They are the descriptive noun-servants, holding up a mirror to them.

Figure 7.2 Adjective illustration

Teaching notes

You will need:

- worksheet
- laminated word cards

Adjective facts

There are many fascinating facts about adjectives that native speakers know unconsciously. Adjectives can be divided into several different classes according to their behaviour and position in a sentence. Additionally to simply being called 'describing words', adjectives are used to modify nouns as shown in the fact list below. This list is intended for your knowledge as a teacher. It can also be used in lessons, should you wish to study adjectives in greater detail.

1 Adjectives can modify nouns or pronouns after the verb *be*:

Birds are feathered.

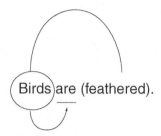

Figure 7.3 Birds are feathered

2 Most adjectives can be modified to express comparative and superlative by adding -er and -est or *more* and *most*.

Sharks are larg**er** than minnows.
Hummingbirds are among the small**est** birds.
Salmon are **more** plentiful in spring.
Crocodiles are the **most** fearsome predators.

The choice of -er/-est as opposed to *more/most* conforms to certain properties contained in the adjectives themselves. There is still some debate about usage in certain cases, but there is also a significant amount of certainty regarding which works best for which adjective. The guidelines generally go like this:

If the adjective is monosyllabic, it will tend to take the er/est form.

thin/thinner/thinnest
young/younger/youngest
old/older/oldest

Adjectives with two syllables are trickier (or more tricky?). Their endings determine the acceptability of er/est. However, some speakers prefer not to use er/est and default to more/most in these circumstances. Which do you do?

If you look at the list, you'll find that many of the candidates come from Old English. The suffixes -er/-est appeared earlier in the language than more/most.

-er   bitter/bitterer/bitterest

- also: clever, dapper, eager, limber, meager [US spelling], sober, somber [US spelling], tender

-le   little/littler/littlest

- also: able, brittle, feeble, fickle, gentle, humble, idle, nimble, noble, purple, simple, supple

-ow   yellow/yellower/yellowest

- also: callow, hollow, mellow, narrow, shallow

-some   handsome/handsomer/handsomest

- also: gruesome, lonesome, toothsome

-y   muddy/muddier/muddiest (employing Return of Illegal <i> – see *Spelling for Life*).

- The list of two syllable -y adjectives is extensive.

Adjectives with more than two syllables tend not to use -er/-est. Syllable number is therefore the most accurate predictor of the correct form.

3 Adjectives can directly follow the word *not.*

Fish are not warm-blooded.
Birds are not cold-blooded.

4 Most adjectives can be modified with emphatic words like *very* and *extremely*:

Blackbirds are very tuneful.
Angel fish are extremely beautiful.

Although some can't:

*Finn wore a very rubber hat.
*An extremely easterly wind blew.
*The dinosaur was very dead.

Those which can't be modified in this way are called non-gradable adjectives. They don't go well with comparative and superlative either, for obvious reasons.

5 Some adjectives cannot be used before a noun.

Carra was aglow.
*An aglow girl.

These are called predicative-only adjectives and often begin with *a-*. Some other predicative-only adjectives:

ablaze, abreast, adrift, afloat, afraid, aghast, alert, alike, alone, aloof, ashamed, asleep, awake, aware

6 Some adjectives can *only* be used before a noun.

The main entrance
*The entrance is main.

These are called attributive-only adjectives. Some other examples:

elder, former, mere, sheer

7 Something that native speakers of English seem to absorb with no effort at all is the general order of adjectives. When there are several being used before a noun, they arrange themselves into a kind of pecking order, encompassing ten or so qualities, and most native speakers have no trouble with it. This general order goes something like:

opinion, size, physical quality, shape, age, colour, origin, material, type, purpose

Figure 7.4 illustrates adjective order. It can be downloaded at https://life-longliteracy.com/free-downloads/

The thing about teaching adjectives

It is a matter for your judgement as to how many aspects of this word class you wish to cover. Native speakers generally already have a good grasp of

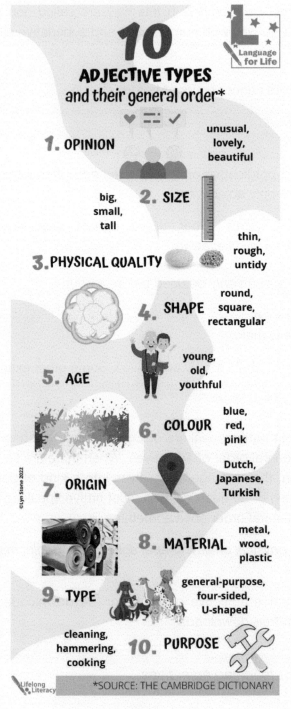

Figure 7.4 Adjective order infographic

the finer points of adjective behaviour and use. There are not many adjective-specific errors in students' writing, so going into the aspects above is really more for linguistic discovery than corrective purposes.

Activities

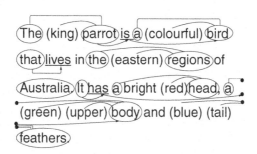

Figure 7.5 Adjective example passage marked

Activity 7.1 Introducing adjectives

Now we have enough parts of speech to construct fully expressive sentences. What are those parts of speech called? (NOUNS, PRONOUNS, AND VERBS)

Let's use some of the nouns, pronouns, and verbs we had in our previous worksheets to make some more sentences.

Have students come up with about five sentences using nouns, pronouns, and verbs only. Write them on the board. They will look something like these:

Shelley swims.
My dragon ate Daryl.
George runs a restaurant.

The point you are trying to make is that using only nouns, pronouns, and verbs is fairly limiting.

Let's take a sentence like:

The eagle ate the fish.

and see what information we have so far.

Who or what are we talking about? (AN EAGLE AND A FISH)

We know what the subject, *eagle*, is doing to the object, *fish*, because we have the verb *ate*.

But if we wanted to say more about the eagle, we could modify it by adding some adjectives. For instance, *majestic*, or *large*. We can really colour our sentences using descriptive words like these. The name for that type of word is *adjective*.

It is often said that adjectives are describing words, but we're going to use a grammatical term that will help us later on. It's the word *modify*. To modify something is to change it in some way. It goes a little further than just describing.

Go to your dragon sentence. What words are modifying the subject, *dragon*? (BIG AND GREEN).

We mark adjectives by putting brackets around them and joining them with a superscript line to the nouns they are modifying. Adjectives modify nouns. Show this on your dragon sentence.

Activity 7.2 – Adjectives and pronouns

Take some of the pronouns from the pronoun lesson and try to place *big* or *green* before them.

For example:

*My big it.
*The green her.

You will discover that pronouns can be used with adjectives if the sentences are constructed a certain way as in:

It was big.
She was green.

If you begin a sentence with a pronoun and use a *be* verb, you can follow this with an adjective.

Activity 7.3 – Test for adjectives

Gather your laminated word cards and construct the following sentences.

1 The _____ statue stood in the park.
2 The mouse was very _____.

The words *small* and *shiny* work in both sentences, but a word like *afraid* only works in sentence 2.

Adjectives worksheet

Marking

Mark adjectives by putting brackets round them.

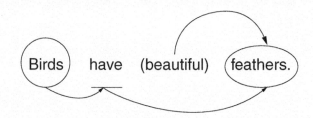

Birds   have   (beautiful)   feathers.

Definition

An adjective is:

_____

_____

_____

Take one of your example sentences and add two more adjectives to the subject.

_____

_____

_____

Lyn Stone (2025), *Language for Life* (2nd Ed.), Routledge

Adjectives example passage

1 Circle the nouns and their determiners.
2 Circle the pronouns.
3 Underline the verbs and draw an arrow from the subject to the verb and the verb to the object if there is one.
4 Put brackets around the adjectives and join them to the words they modify.

The king parrot is a colourful bird that lives in the eastern regions of Australia. It has a bright red head, a green upper body and blue tail feathers.

Lyn Stone (2025), *Language for Life* (2nd Ed.), Routledge

8 Adverbs

The flying squad

Definition

Adverbs describe, add information to, or modify verbs, adjectives, clauses, and other adverbs.

Etymology

Latin *ad-* 'to' + *verb* 'word' → adverb

Marking

Adverbs in our example sentences will also be bracketed, with superscript lines joining the elements they modify.

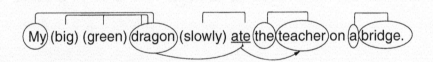

My (big) (green) dragon (slowly) ate the teacher on a bridge.

Figure 8.1 Adverb dragon sentence marked

DOI: 10.4324/9781003457930-8

Story

Adverbs are also used for modification, but are not in the exclusive service of nouns. We call them the Flying Squad because they can change their position in sentences and work to modify all kinds of words, phrases and even whole sentences.

Figure 8.2 Adverb illustration

Teaching notes

As we found out in the previous chapter, adjectives modify nouns and pronouns. However, adjectives themselves can also be modified, as can verbs, whole clauses, and adverbs themselves. Welcome to the Flying Squad.[1]

Myth

Adverbs describe verbs and end in -ly.

Adverbs are not as straightforward as the preceding parts of speech, in that they can function in a number of ways, depending on what they are modifying. They also don't always end in -ly, although this is a handy signal in some cases.

The following lessons will introduce adverbs, then take the word class most commonly associated with adverbs, the verbs, first and work our way through the lesser-known functions.

Whereas we could alter the form of nouns (e.g. singular/plural), verbs (e.g. tense/case/voice), and adjectives (e.g. comparative/superlative), adverbs are

---

1 In UK English, the Flying Squad was a specialist police division authorised to operate anywhere in London, rather than within divisional boundaries. So it is with adverbs, in that they can modify several different parts of speech and can occupy many different positions in sentences.

the first word class that cannot be altered. As the lesson proceeds, you will begin to notice this phenomenon.

From now on, in fact, each part of speech (adverbs, prepositions, and conjunctions) often have this 'unalterable' characteristic.

Adverbs worksheet notes

Common question

Q. Why isn't *were* in the phrase *were busily making* marked as having a subject or an object?

A. *Were* is an auxiliary verb, going with *making*. Adverbs can be inserted between auxiliary and main verbs.

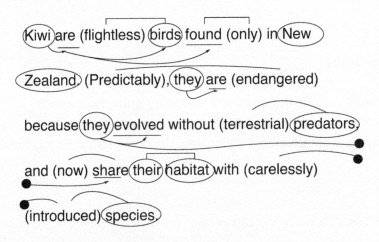

Figure 8.3 Adverb example passage marked

Activities

Activity 8.1 – Discovering adverbs

There are other descriptive words in our language. We're going to look at some now. We've already added more information to our nouns, now let's add to the verbs and other parts of speech.

Let's look at our dragon sentence and see what word goes just before the verb. What's the verb in this sentence? (ATE)

What is the word directly before it? (SLOWLY)

What job is the word *slowly* doing here? (MODIFYING THE VERB)
We call this an adverb.
Let's write the first part of the definition.

Definition

An adverb is a word that modifies a verb.

Activity 8.2 – Adverbs and word order

We can also put the adverb at the end of the sentence. So we could say:

My big green dragon ate the teacher on a bridge slowly.

Have students review their own sentences to find adverbs. Ask them to select one sentence with an adverb and see if they can place it in a different spot in the sentence.

Some students may have sentences with no adverbs. Ask them to select a sentence, add an adverb, and then change its position in the sentence.

Activity 8.3 – Modifying adjectives

Also, if we said *very big green dragon* in the example sentence, what job would you say *very* is doing? (MODIFYING *BIG*)
  Adverbs can also modify adjectives. Let's add that to the definition.

Definition

An adverb is a word that modifies a verb. Adverbs can also modify adjectives.

Activity 8.4 – Modifying adverbs

Also, if we said *very slowly* at the end of the example sentence, what job would you say *very* is doing? (MODIFYING *SLOWLY*)
  Adverbs can also modify other adverbs. Let's add that to the definition.

Definition

An adverb is a word that modifies a verb. Adverbs can also modify adjectives and other adverbs.

Activity 8.5 – Common adverb ending

Many of these adverbs end with the same suffix: *-ly*. You can often spot an adverb because it ends with this suffix.

Let's think of another *-ly* word that could go in place of *slowly* in the dragon sentence.

Let the students suggest other *-ly* words.

Activity 8.6 – Adverbs modifying verbs

Have students turn to their adverbs worksheet. You will show some worked examples of adverbs modifying certain parts of speech and sentence parts and then get them to write and mark some examples.

1 Adverbs can add various kinds of descriptive information to other words. For instance, in the following sentences, what kind of information is the adverb providing?

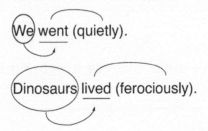

Figure 8.4 Adverbs of manner

These adverbs show *how* something is or happens. We call this *manner*. Adverbs of manner are often formed by adding the adverb-forming suffix -ly to an adjective.

2 What do the following adverbs show?

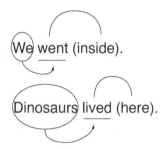

Figure 8.5 Adverbs of place

Answer: these adverbs show where something is or happens. We call this *place*.

3 What do the following adverbs show?

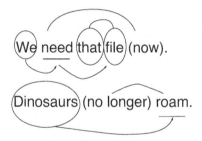

Figure 8.6 Adverbs of time

Answer: These adverbs show when something is or happens. We call this *time*.

4 What do the following adverbs show?

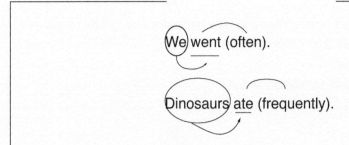

Figure 8.7 Adverbs of frequency

Answer: the adverbs above show how often something happened. We call this *frequency*.

Activity 8.7 – Adverb + verb flexibility

Nouns, verbs, and adjectives have a fairly rigid system of order. We tend to start sentences with subjects, go to verbs, and then to objects. Adjectives follow determiners and mostly go before nouns. If they go after verbs, they are quite specific too.

One thing that sets adverbs apart is that they have mobility. Look at this model, for example. We can use the adverb *carefully* in every position in a simple subject–verb–object sentence.

1. (possible adverb),   2. (possible adverb), 3. (possible adverb),   4. (possible adverb),

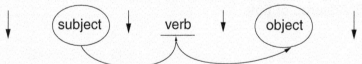

  1. Carefully, the dog ate the turkey.
  2. The dog carefully ate the turkey.
  3. The dog ate, carefully, the turkey.
  4. The dog ate the turkey carefully.

Figure 8.8 Possible adverb positions

Use of commas in 1 and 3 is required, and there is a slightly different emphasis in 3, but the overall meaning doesn't change significantly. Out of *manner*, *place*, *time*, and *frequency*, manner is the most flexible.

Activity 8.8 – Adverbs modifying adjectives

When adverbs modify adjectives, they are usually stating degree, i.e. how much of whatever quality the adjective is expressing. For example:

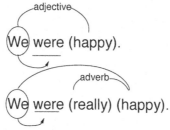

Figure 8.9 Adverbs modifying adjectives

Some other adverbs of degree:
about, absolutely, almost, around, completely, enough (e.g. *This dinosaur is big enough*), extremely, just, quite, so, sort of, very

Activity 8.9 – Adverbs modifying other adverbs

We can use adverbs of degree to intensify adverbs already employed in the task of modifying verbs.

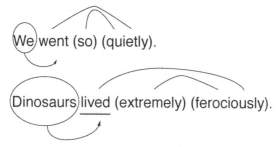

Figure 8.10 Adverbs modifying adverbs

Activity 8.10 – Adverbs modifying clauses

Additionally, when an adverb is placed at the beginning of a sentence or a clause, it places emphasis on the particular manner, time, place or frequency of that clause. In other positions, this emphasis is less. In cases where the adverb is first in the clause, it could be said that the adverb is modifying the entire clause. Consider:

> Honestly, *I don't know why people are so uptight about grammar.*
> Clearly, *you've never seen an example of good manners before.*
> Ideally, *the sun would shine by day and it would rain at night.*

If we took the adverbs above and put them elsewhere in our sentences, not at the beginning, their meanings would be slightly different. Compare the sentences above with the following:

> *I cannot* honestly *take any money from you.*
> *The child saw* clearly *after the surgery.*
> *The house is* ideally *situated.*

Use the worksheet to select three sentence adverbs and show contrasting sentences.

Adverbs example sentence

To note that we have spotted an adverb in a sentence, we will put brackets around it just like we did for adjectives. Why do you think we use the same marking for adjectives and adverbs? (THEY BOTH MODIFY.)

Adverbs worksheet

Definition

An adverb is:

_____

_____

_____

Sentence adverbs

Choose three adverbs from the list below and write one sentence that begins with a sentence adverb. Then use the adverb again, but this time not at the beginning of the sentence. For example:

1 Seriously, does anyone even watch TV any more?
2 The driver was seriously injured.

Adverb list

apparently, basically, briefly, certainly, clearly, confidentially, curiously, evidently, happily, honestly, hopefully, however, ideally, incidentally, ironically, naturally, presumably, regrettably, sadly, seriously, strangely, surprisingly, thankfully, theoretically, ultimately, unfortunately

_____

_____

_____

_____

_____

_____

_____

_____

_____

Lyn Stone (2025), *Language for Life* (2nd Ed.), Routledge

Adverbs example sentences

Take one of your example sentences and add two more adverbs.

_____

_____

_____

Adverbs example passage

1 Circle the nouns and their determiners.
2 Circle the pronouns.
3 Underline the verbs and draw an arrow from the subject to the verb and the verb to the object if there is one.
4 Put brackets around the adjectives and connect them to the words they modify.
5 Put brackets around the adverbs and connect them to the words they modify.

Kiwi are flightless birds found only in New

Zealand. Predictably, they are endangered

because they evolved without terrestrial predators,

and now share their habitat with carelessly

introduced species.

Lyn Stone (2025), *Language for Life* (2nd Ed.), Routledge

Parts of speech progress check

Two-thirds of the lessons on parts of speech have now been completed. Your students are familiar with subjects, verbs, objects, and words which modify them. All that is left are the relationship words: those with the task of knitting elements of sentences together.

Each relationship word has its own special way of uniting the words around it. Some show location, some show time. Some show how whole sentences are more or less important than other whole sentences.

Words in this category are called prepositions and conjunctions.

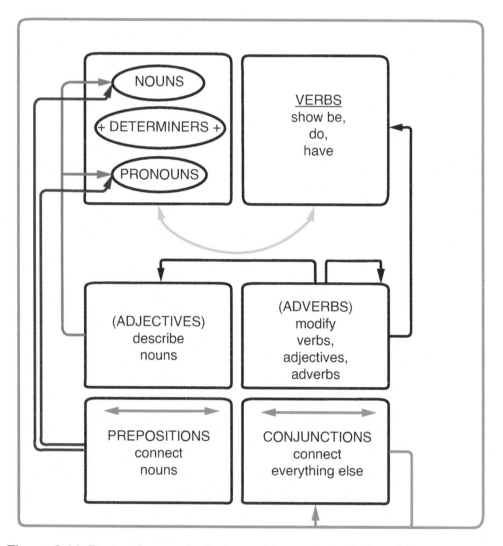

Figure 8.11 Parts of speech, their markings, and relationships

9 Prepositions

Noun connectors

Definition

Prepositions connect nouns to other sentence parts. They are often small function words, but can also be phrases.

Etymology

pre + pose + ite + ion → preposition

Marking

Prepositions will be marked with a superscript, double-headed arrow. We won't use arrows to show relationships between prepositions and other parts of the sentence, as this can get extremely complex very quickly.

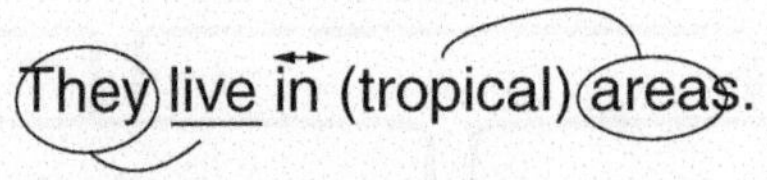

They live in (tropical) areas.

Figure 9.1 Preposition marking example

DOI: 10.4324/9781003457930-9

Preposition story

Prepositions are the next set of noun-servants. They connect their nouns with other parts of sentences. They do this by showing us what kind of relationship the royal nouns have with the other words.

Figure 9.2 Preposition illustration

Teaching notes

Myth and counter-myth

'Prepositions are words which show position, like *behind, under* etc.' Though this is somewhat their role, it's not their complete role.

Prepositions are yet another noun-servant. The job of a preposition is to show very specific information about the relationship a noun has with the other elements in a clause. It is always about nouns and their relationships.

Prepositions showing position are common and easy to spot, as in:

They live **in** *tropical areas.*

However, there are many more ways in which prepositions connect nouns to other elements.

As an introduction, you can look at some common additional preposition roles by a 'preposition swap', where you place a different preposition in an example sentence and see how the meaning changes. Also note how it changes the relationship of the noun to the rest of the sentence. You can do this as much or as little as needed to get the idea across to your students.

Direction

 around, beside, by, from, in, into, on, onto past, to, up

The birds flew _____ the cage.

Instrument

 with, without

The birds flew _____ their wings.

Manner

 with, without

The birds flew _____ confidence.

Possession

 of

The birds of Africa migrate.

Position

 alongside, above, below, beneath, between, in, near, next to, opposite, under, underneath

The birds live _____ the trees.

Purpose

 for

The birds fought for survival.

Source

 of, from, out of

The birds are made _____ wood.

Duration

 during, since, within

The birds flew/have flown _____ winter.

Special note on the word of

We need to deal with a very common preposition, and indeed one of the most common words in our language: the word *of*.

Some prepositions are easy to spot: *behind, under, near* etc., but *of* is trickier.

The Concise Oxford Dictionary gives it nine definitions, but sums its function up thus: 'Preposition connecting its noun with preceding noun, adjective, adverb or verb and indicating relations . . .'

Prepositions and nuance

Some sentences can dramatically change in meaning just by virtue of the preposition. Would you rather be laughed *with* or *at*? It's better that someone is afraid *for* you or afraid *of* you?

Prepositions worksheet notes

Nouns and prepositions

Fill in the correct preposition from the two choices.

concern	for (of/for)
respect	of (of/for)
grasp	of (of/for)
participation	in (at/in)

Adjectives and prepositions

Fill in the correct preposition from the two choices.

angry	at (at/of)
worried	for (of/for)
similar	to (from/to)
proud	of (of/for)
interested	in (of/in)
capable	of (to/of)
jealous	of (of/for)
sorry	for (of/for)

Verbs and prepositions

Fill in the correct preposition from the two choices.

apologise	for (of/for)
trust	in (in/at)
belong	to (to/at)
worry	for (of/for)
study	for (of/for)
prepare	for (of/for)

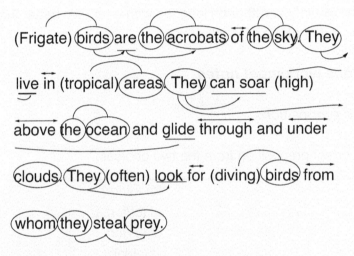

(Frigate) birds are the acrobats of the sky. They live in (tropical) areas. They can soar (high) above the ocean and glide through and under clouds. They (often) look for (diving) birds from whom they steal prey.

Figure 9.3 Preposition example passage marked

Activities

Activity 9.1 – Preposition introduction

Our sentences are now pretty colourful. We can describe nouns, pronouns, and verbs with adjectives and adverbs.

The last two parts of speech that we are going to learn about also have similar jobs.

When we communicate, we often need to join our ideas together. We use our language like building blocks, one idea with another, either by showing how one word relates to another, or even how one sentence relates to another.

We are going to look at particular words which show the relationship between words or even join sentences and words to whole other sentences. These words are the relationship words. Let's take the ones that join nouns first.

We've looked at and marked the example sentence:

My big green dragon slowly ate the teacher on a bridge.

So we have two nouns and their determiners, a pronoun and a noun, two adjectives, an adverb, and a word in the sentence we haven't marked yet. What word? (ON)

What is the word *on* doing in this sentence? (IT IS SHOWING WHERE THE DRAGON ATE THE TEACHER.)

What parts of speech are linked by the preposition in this sentence? (THE VERB *ATE*, THE NOUNS *DRAGON*, *TEACHER*, AND *BRIDGE*.)

That's right, this tiny word *on* unites all the main parts of the sentence with the noun where everything took place. Prepositions might sometimes be small, they don't stand out as the subject or object, they don't add shades of descriptive colour, but the job they do is just as important as all the others.

Let's write the definition.

We're going to mark prepositions in our sentences by putting a double-headed arrow over the top of them.

Ask students to turn to their worksheets and write the following:

A preposition is a word that shows a noun's relationship to other words and phrases.

They should then review their own sentences for prepositions and discuss the parts of speech that are united by those prepositions.

If their sentences do not contain any prepositions, guide them to select and use some from the list in Table 9.1.

Table 9.1 Place prepositions list

above	across	against
among	at	behind
beneath	beside	between
beyond	by	from
in	in front of	next to
off	on	over
through	under	upon
with	within	without

Activity 9.2 – Of in all of its glory

There is a very common preposition in our language. This is the word *of*.

Here are some example sentences. Think about the noun relationships that the word *of* is showing:

The frigate bird is one of the highest flying seabirds.
The frigate bird is chasing a pair of gulls.

Of is one of our oldest words and is used to show relations between nouns and other words in many different ways. When you see it, you are going to mark it as a preposition.

As we saw before, prepositions show how nouns connect to other words.

Let's make a note.

NOTE: The word OF is a preposition. It connects nouns.

Activity 9.3 – Strong bonds

Suggested dialogue

Some words are so strongly bonded to certain prepositions that they sound very strange with an incorrect one. Consider:

*Joanne doesn't believe for ghosts.

What should the preposition be? (IN)
  Sometimes it's not that easy to decide on the correct preposition. Some words can dramatically change a sentence's meaning just by virtue of the preposition it is bonded to. Would you rather be laughed *with* or *at*? It's better that someone is afraid *for* you or afraid *of* you?
  Your worksheet has some exercises in/on this. Which one? (THIS IS OPEN TO DEBATE)

Students fill in the missing prepositions and discuss their different choices.

Prepositions worksheet

Definition

A preposition is a word which:

_____

_____

_____

Examples

1 _____

2 _____

3 _____

4 _____

Note

_____

_____

Nouns and prepositions

Fill in the correct preposition from the two choices and write a sentence with
your phrase.

_____

concern _____ (of/for)

respect _____ (of/for)

grasp _____ (of/for)

participation _____ (at/in)

_____

Lyn Stone (2025), *Language for Life* (2nd Ed.), Routledge

Adjectives and prepositions

Fill in the correct preposition from the two choices

angry	_____	(at/of)
worried	_____	(of/for)
similar	_____	(from/to)
proud	_____	(of/for)
interested	_____	(of/in)
capable	_____	(to/of)
jealous	_____	(of/for)
sorry	_____	(of/for)

Verbs and prepositions

Fill in the correct preposition from the two choices.

apologise	_____	(of/for)
trust	_____	(in/at)
belong	_____	(to/at)
worry	_____	(of/for)
study	_____	(of/for)
prepare	_____	(of/for)

Prepositions example sentence

Now take one of your example sentences and add a preposition and some more information.

_____

_____

_____

Lyn Stone (2025), *Language for Life* (2nd Ed.), Routledge

Example passage

1 Circle the nouns and their determiners.
2 Circle the pronouns.
3 Underline the verbs and draw an arrow from the subject to the verb and the verb to the object if there is one.
4 Put brackets around the adjectives and connect them to the words they modify.
5 Put brackets around the adverbs and connect them to the words they modify.
6 Put a double-headed arrow on top of the prepositions.

Frigate birds are the acrobats of the sky. They

live in tropical areas. They can soar high

above the ocean and glide through and under

clouds. They often look for diving birds from

whom they steal prey.

Lyn Stone (2025), *Language for Life* (2nd Ed.), Routledge

Extension activity – Complex prepositions

Suggested dialogue

Aside from strongly bonded prepositions, complex prepositions contain a whole string of up to four words. This brings us quite neatly up to phrases in the next lesson, but for now, consider the use of the following complex prepositions:

on behalf of
such as
in order to
for the sake of
by means of
as opposed to

Can you think of any more?

10 Conjunctions
All-round joiners

Definition

A conjunction is a word that connects not only individual words, but larger parts of sentences to one another. By larger parts we mean phrases, clauses, and sentences, not just words.

Etymology

con + junct (join) + ion → conjunction

Marking

Like prepositions, conjunctions will be marked with a two-headed arrow sitting above them.

Story

Conjunctions are like air-traffic controllers. They are words words that connect not only individual words, but larger parts of sentences to one another. By larger parts we mean phrases, clauses and sentences, not just words. These are the all-round joiners.

Figure 10.1 Conjunction illustration

DOI: 10.4324/9781003457930-10

Teaching notes

Conjunction types

There are three main conjunction types:

- coordinating conjunctions (e.g. *or, and*, *but*)
- subordinating conjunctions (e.g. *until, because, whether*)
- correlative conjunctions (e.g. *not only . . . but also, neither . . . nor, whether . . . or*).

You and your students will explore each type.

Conjunctions constitute a closed, non-alterable word class. Below is a table of common single-word conjunctions designating their type.

Table 10.1 Conjunctions

Type	Function	Examples
Coordinating conjunctions	To join elements that have equal status in a sentence	for, and, nor, but, or, yet, so (FANBOYS)
Subordinating conjunctions	To join subordinate clauses to main clauses	although, because, if, unless, until
Correlative conjunctions	These join sentence elements in the same way as coordinating conjunctions, but function as a pair	both . . . and, either . . . or, neither . . . nor, whether . . . or, not only . . . but also

Additional subordinating conjunctions

after	in order for/that	though
as	lest	till (or 'til)
as long as	now that	when
as soon as/no sooner than	once	whenever
as though	provided (that)	where
because	since	whereas
before	so that	wherever
even if	than	whether
even though	that	while

You may have noticed that some of the words listed have appeared in chapters about other parts of speech. This is not an error, but a fine example of the fact that *function* determines category. What a word can be labelled as is often dependent on its relationship with other words in context.

Furthermore, in the world of conjunctions, we edge ever closer to the world of phrases and clauses, where multiple words are bound together to perform a single function. For example, the phrase 'as long as' consists of three words, but could easily be replaced by a single conjunction, such as 'because' or 'while':

As long as there are fish in the river, the eagle can eat.
While there are fish in the river, the eagle can eat.

Coordinating conjunction

Birds fly but some don't.

Subordinating conjunction

Stilts are called stilts because they have long legs.
Because they have long legs, stilts are called stilts.

Correlative conjunction

Crows eat not only meat but also plants and vegetables.
The mantis shrimp is neither a mantis nor a shrimp.

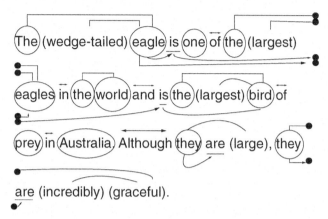

Figure 10.2 Conjunction example passage marked

Activities

Activity 10.1 – Discovering conjunctions

Sometimes when we are talking or writing, we like to say more than just
one idea in one sentence at a time. If we talked only in complete sentences that had one subject, one verb, what do you think our speech
and writing would be like? (BORING AND STILTED ARE SOME OF THE
POSSIBLE ANSWERS HERE)

Let's take the example passage:

The wedge-tailed eagle is one of the largest eagles in the world and is
the largest bird of prey in Australia. Although they are large, they are
incredibly graceful.

In the first sentence, there are two main ideas: first is that wedge-tailed
eagles are some of the largest eagles in the world, and second that they
are the largest bird of prey in Australia.

Which word joins those ideas together? (AND)

A word that joins ideas like this is called a conjunction. Write the definition:

A conjunction is a word or phrase that joins other words and phrases together.

The second sentence is also in two parts but this time, we can take the part that begins with the conjunction 'although' and put it after the second part, like so:

They are incredibly graceful although they are large.

When we can change the order like this, we know we have a main clause and a subordinate clause. Subordinating conjunctions connect subordinate clauses to main clauses. We will discover more about clauses in the following chapters. What we need to discuss here is that when subordinate and main clauses go together, they form *complex sentences*. The conjunctions are used to join them by showing time, place, or cause. Think about this sentence:

The eagle chick might fledge if the wind stops blowing.

We have the main clause *The eagle chick might fledge*, the subordinating conjunction *if*, and then the subordinate clause *if the wind stops blowing*.

Subordinate clauses are named this way because they make sense when attached to a main clause. It wouldn't make sense to simply say or write **If the wind stops blowing.*

Activity 10.2 – Coordinating conjunctions

We looked at the word *and*, which we agreed made two elements in the sentence equal. The name for this type of conjunction is *coordinating conjunction*. When two clauses are joined by a coordinating conjunction, this is called a compound sentence.

The seven major coordinating conjunctions can be remembered with a simple acronym: FANBOYS
This stands for:

for, and, nor, but, or, yet, so

We mark conjunctions by putting a two-headed arrow above them.

Activity 10.3 – Correlative conjunctions

Some conjunctions combine with other words to form a pair. These are called *correlative conjunctions*. They always appear together, joining various sentence elements. They should be treated as coordinating conjunctions.

1 The eagle *not only* eats fish, *but also* rabbits. Note: it is also acceptable to say *not only . . . but . . .*, omitting the word *also* in longer constructions.
2 The wedge-tailed eagle is *neither* an endangered *nor* a threatened species.
3 *Whether* in the tropical north or in the cool south, wedge-tailed eagles can be found all over Australia.

Have students suggest possible additions to the example sentence and join them with some of the conjunctions studied so far. For example:

Coordinating conjunction

My big green dragon slowly ate the teacher on a bridge but left her hat behind.

Subordinating conjunction

My big green dragon slowly ate the teacher on a bridge after she finally caught her.

Correlative conjunction

Either my big green dragon slowly ate the teacher on a bridge or I'm imagining things.

Conjunctions worksheet

1 Definition. A conjunction is:

_____

_____

_____

_____

2 Add more information by using the three types of conjunction at the end of this sentence:

Coordinating conjunction

My big green dragon slowly ate the teacher on a bridge

_____

_____

Subordinating conjunction

My big green dragon slowly ate the teacher on a bridge

_____

_____

Correlative conjunction

My big green dragon slowly ate the teacher on a bridge

_____

_____

3 Now take one of your example sentences and add a conjunction and some more information.

_____

_____

_____

Lyn Stone (2025), *Language for Life* (2nd Ed.), Routledge

4 Choose three coordinating conjunctions and three subordinating conjunctions and use them in sentences. Make sure you can clearly show coordination and subordination.

Lyn Stone (2025), *Language for Life* (2nd Ed.), Routledge

Conjunctions example passage

1 Circle the nouns and their determiners and connect them with a superscript line.
2 Circle the pronouns.
3 Underline the verbs and draw a subscript arrow from the subject to the verb and the verb to the object if there is one.
4 Put brackets around the adjectives and connect them to the words they modify.
5 Put brackets around the adverbs and connect them to the words they modify.
6 Put a double-headed arrow around the prepositions.
7 Put a double-headed arrow around the conjunctions.

The wedge-tailed eagle is one of the largest

eagles in the world and is the largest bird of

prey in Australia. Although they are large, they

are incredibly graceful.

Lyn Stone (2025), *Language for Life* (2nd Ed.), Routledge

Parts of speech final progress check

The major parts of speech have now been covered. Figure 10.3 shows each word class and also some extra information about whether the classes are:

- alterable or unalterable (plurals, tense, case, comparison) and
- closed or open (i.e. whether they constitute a finite set or whether new examples can be added).

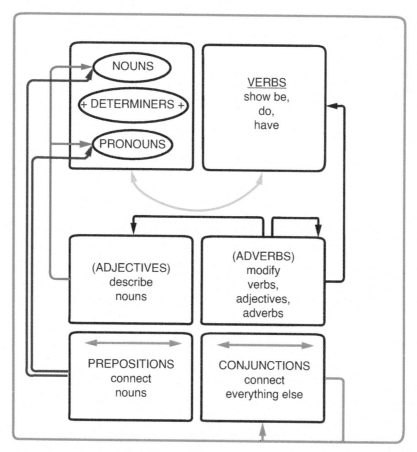

Figure 10.3 Parts of speech, their markings, and their relationships

11 Phrases

A phrase is a unit in a sentence that functions as a whole within a larger construction.

When is a sentence not a sentence? When is a clause not a clause? Well, when it's a phrase. A phrase can be one of several things:

- a subject
- a verb
- an object
- another word or group of words relating to the subject, the verb or the object.

Phrases NEVER contain a subject AND an object. That would be a clause. We'll deal with clauses after this.

In music, phrasing gives expression and meaning to tunes and songs. In language, phrasing gives structure and variety to our communication.

We are naturally aware of phrasing, tending to group words around those essential elements, the nouns and verbs. Consider the act of dictating the following sentence.

The sloth pulled itself up in the tall tree.

Dictation forces us to slow down and pause, yet we still tend to dictate in phrases, whether we are aware of it or not. We would tend not to say:

The sloth pulled
. . . . itself up in . . .
the tall . . .
tree.

But rather:

The sloth . . .
pulled itself up . . .
in the tall tree.

DOI: 10.4324/9781003457930-11

A phrase can be one word, such as *they* in:

They released the kiwi into the forest.

In this sentence, *they* is the subject and is also a phrase. There are other phrases in the sentence:

the kiwi into the forest.

which is the object of the verb *released*. This phrase includes the smaller phrases *into the forest* and *the forest*.

If we were to analyse linguistic units from the sub-word to the paragraph level, phrases would come just after words and before clauses.

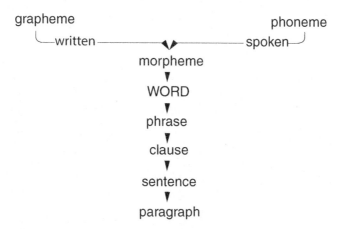

Figure 11.1 Sub-word to paragraph units

In linguistics, sentences are often illustrated using phrase-structure trees. These trees provide a fascinating visual analysis of the internal structure of sentences. Take the sentence:

Ken watches cartoons on a Saturday.

This sentence can be represented by the following simple tree diagram.

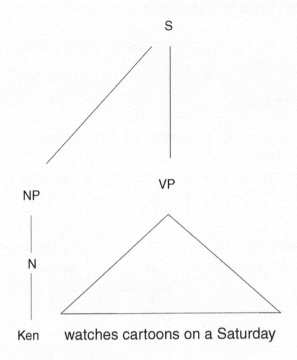

Figure 11.2 Simple Ken tree

Key:

S = sentence
N = noun
NP = noun phrase
VP = verb phrase

Just above the word-level we have phrases. These phrases are termed 'constituents' in linguistics, which is what is meant by 'constituent analysis' – another way of talking about phrase structure.

We could take that whole triangle, representing *watches cartoons on a Saturday*, and replace it with one word, such as *sleeps* or *yawns* or *stretches*. What we can also do is analyse the verb phrase further, breaking it down into its constituents. The words which group themselves together naturally are *watches cartoons* and *on a Saturday*. Now the tree would look like this:

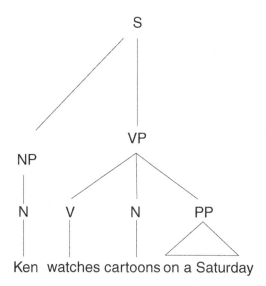

Figure 11.3 Less simple Ken tree

If we were to analyse the sentence even further, we would see that the prepositional phrase (PP), *on a Saturday* contains a preposition (Prep) and a noun phrase (NP).

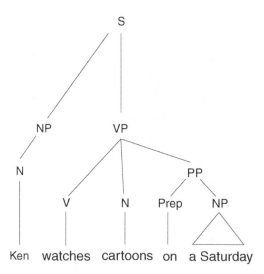

Figure 11.4 Less simple Ken tree 2

At its most complex, the noun phrase can be broken down into a noun and a determiner (Det), giving us the least simple version of this sentence's phrase-structure tree below.

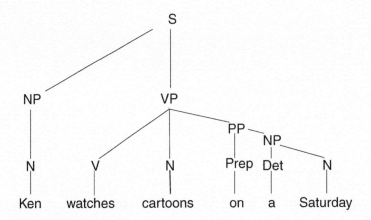

Figure 11.5 Least simple Ken tree

Drawing phrase-structure trees takes time and thought and can be as complex as the sentences they reflect. It is not a recommended activity in the classroom, but, rather, is mentioned here for teacher knowledge.

12 Clauses

Definition

A clause, in its simplest sense, is a group of words containing at least one subject and one verb.

Etymology

Latin *claudere*, 'to close, shut, conclude'

Teaching notes

A clause can either stand alone as a complete sentence or it can be included in a string of multiple clauses. In the case of multiple clauses, there must always be a stand-alone main one.

There are two types of clause:

1 Independent clauses a.k.a. main clauses. Every sentence contains at least one main clause.
2 Dependent clauses a.k.a. subordinate clauses. They cannot stand on their own and depend on a main clause to make sense.

When added together in certain ways, they form either compound or complex sentences.

Coordination vs. subordination

Clauses are often joined together by conjunctions. There are two distinct clause types, depending on the kind of conjunction used. Compare the two sentences below.

1) The king parrot ate the seeds but it was not hungry.
2) The king parrot ate the seeds although it was not hungry.

DOI: 10.4324/9781003457930-12

The 'but' conjunction in 1) indicates coordination between the two clauses. It would be perfectly fine to drop the pronoun 'it' when the clauses are coordinated:

1a) The king parrot ate the seeds but was not hungry.

On the other hand, leaving out the preposition in 2) is ungrammatical:

*1b) The king parrot ate the seeds although was not hungry.

The other sign of coordination is flexibility of position. We can move the entire subordinate clause to the front of the sentence and still have a grammatical utterance:

2c) Although it was not hungry, the king parrot ate the seeds.
*1c) But it was not hungry the king parrot ate the seeds.

Notice how well a comma works after a sentence-first subordinate clause.

Clauses worksheet notes

Independent (main) clauses

1 Write the list of common coordinating conjunctions under the acronym.

F	A	N	B	O	Y	S
for	and	nor	but	or	yet	so

2 Underline the first independent clause and write the coordinating conjunction underneath.

a <u>My plane was late</u> and the snowstorm was fierce.

and

b <u>The aphids were sprayed</u> but they still attacked the plant.

but

c <u>The teacher had a piano for sale</u> so she put an ad in the paper.

so

3 Combine each of the two sentences below to make one compound sentence (clue: you'll have to use a coordinating conjunction).

    a The brolga doesn't migrate but it covers wide distances.

    b Brolgas tend to want to impress their mates so they do elaborate courtship dances.

    c Brolgas suffer from habitat loss and they suffer from fox predation.

Dependent (subordinate) clauses

1 Underline the subordinate clauses in the following sentences and write the subordinating conjunction underneath:

    a <u>Unless an Isa Brown hen is old or sick</u>, she will lay an egg almost every day.
      unless

    b Hens are best kept in pairs or groups <u>because they are social creatures.</u>
      because

    c Keeping Isa Brown hens is best <u>until you are very good at caring for chickens.</u>
      until

Activities

Activity 12.1 – Defining clauses

Now we know what phrases are, we are going to look at what happens when you join phrases together. There is just one more sentence part that we need to look at: clauses. Let's start with a definition.

DEFINITION: A clause is a group of words containing at least one subject and one verb.

Activity 12.2 – Independent clauses

Write the following sentence:

Ravens usually raise two chicks per year but they can raise three chicks at a time.

We have two main ideas here, what are they?

(1 THAT RAVENS USUALLY RAISE TWO CHICKS PER YEAR.
2 THAT RAVENS CAN RAISE THREE CHICKS AT A TIME.)

Neither of them relies on the other for their meaning. They are both independent clauses joined with the coordinating conjunction, *but*. What we have here, then, is a *compound sentence*:

independent clause + independent clause = compound sentence

One of the ways to tell if you have a compound sentence is that you can do away with the subject in the second clause and it would still make sense:

Ravens usually raise two chicks per year but can raise three chicks at a time.

Activity 12.3 – Coordinating conjunctions

Independent clauses can be separated from one another by coordinating conjunctions. We looked at this in the lesson on conjunctions.
  If we break the word *coordinate* down, we find this:

co + ordin ('order') + ate → coordinate

So here the word *coordinate* is a verb meaning 'arranged together' as opposed to 'subordinate' meaning 'arranged under'. Coordinate clauses are joined by coordinating conjunctions.
  Here is a list of common coordinating conjunctions and a trick to remember them:

F A N B O Y S
for and nor but or yet so

They are not the only coordinating conjunctions in existence, but are a good guide to the type of words you can use for this purpose.

Students practise spotting and defining the clauses in compound sentences on their worksheet.

Activity 12.4 – Dependent clauses

Another name for a dependent clause is *subordinate clause*. The word *subordinate* is made from three parts: a prefix, a base, and a suffix:

sub + ordin + ate → subordinate

Anything that is subordinate is less powerful or of a lower order than something else. I've heard someone say that subordinate clauses are like Batman: pretty good but has to rely on all his gadgets. Independent clauses, on the other hand are like Superman: they can do anything, all with their own power.

Subordinate clauses act as modifiers of a main clause, and therefore rely on a main clause to make sense

Activity 12.5 – Subordinating conjunctions

Let's look at the example sentence again with one difference: this time we are using a subordinating conjunction.

Ravens usually raise two chicks per year although they can raise three chicks at a time.

What word makes the second clause dependent or subordinate? (THE CONJUNCTION *ALTHOUGH*)

Subordinate clauses are dependent because they contain words that make them that way. Those words are called subordinating conjunctions.

Instead of saying the sentence that way, I could take out the subordinating conjunction and have two independent clauses. If I did that, how would I write it? (RAVENS USUALLY RAISE TWO CHICKS PER YEAR. THEY CAN RAISE THREE CHICKS AT A TIME.)

I'd have to make it into two sentences. It wouldn't sound right if I just ran one clause into the other. Sometimes people keep the whole thing as one sentence, but they separate the dependent and independent clauses by using a semicolon instead of a subordinating word like because, like this:

> *Ravens usually raise two chicks per year; they can raise three chicks at a time.*

More about that in our lessons on punctuation.

One characteristic of subordination compared to coordination is that this time you cannot leave out the subject in the second clause:

> ** Ravens usually raise two chicks per year although can raise three chicks at a time.*

This time we have a different kind of sentence.

Have students write this formula

main clause + subordinate clause = complex sentence

Activity 12.6 – Reversal

One more exciting thing that you can do with subordinate clauses is reversal. Consider:

> *Ravens usually raise two chicks per year although they can raise three chicks at a time.*
> *Although they can raise three chicks at a time, ravens usually raise two chicks per year.*

When you start your sentence with a dependent clause, it's a good idea to separate the clauses out with a comma.

Let's have a look at the conjunctions table again and do the exercises on the worksheet:

Table 12.1 Conjunctions

Type	Function	Examples
Coordinating conjunctions	To join elements that have equal status in a sentence	for, and, nor, but, or, yet, so (FANBOYS)
Subordinating conjunctions	To join subordinate clauses to main clauses	although, because, if, unless, until
Correlative conjunctions	These join sentence elements in the same way as coordinating conjunctions, but function as a pair	both . . . and, either . . . or, neither . . . nor, whether . . . or, not only . . . but also

Additional subordinating conjunctions

after	in order for/that	though
as	lest	till (or 'til)
as long as	now that	when
as soon as/no sooner than	once	whenever
as though	provided (that)	where
because	since	whereas
before	so that	wherever
even if	than	whether
even though	that	while

Clauses worksheet

Independent (main) clauses

1 Write the list of common coordinating conjunctions under the acronym

F	A	N
_____	_____	_____

B	O	Y	S
_____	_____	_____	_____

2 Underline the first independent clause and write the coordinating conjunction underneath.

   a My plane was late and the snowstorm was fierce.

   _____

   b The aphids were sprayed but they still attacked the plant.

   _____

   c The teacher had a piano for sale so she put an ad in the paper.

   _____

3 Combine each of the two sentences below to make one compound sentence (clue: you'll have to use a coordinating conjunction).

   a The brolga doesn't migrate. The brolga covers wide distances.

   _____

   _____

   b Brolgas tend to want to impress their mates. They do elaborate courtship dances.

   _____

   _____

Lyn Stone (2025), *Language for Life* (2nd Ed.), Routledge

c   Brolgas suffer from habitat loss. Brolgas suffer from fox predation.

_____

_____

Dependent (subordinate) clauses

1 Underline the subordinate clauses in the following sentences and write the subordinating conjunction underneath.

a Unless an Isa Brown hen is old or sick, she will lay an egg almost every day.

_____

b Hens are best kept in pairs or groups because they are social creatures.

_____

c Keeping Isa Brown hens is best until you are very good at caring for chickens.

_____

Lyn Stone (2025), *Language for Life* (2nd Ed.), Routledge

13 Sentences

Sentences are one of the linchpins of the writing system. Like reading comprehension, sentence construction should be a major goal of literacy teaching. This is where phonological awareness, letter formation, sound symbol knowledge, pen grip, posture, paper position, spelling, grammar, syntax, punctuation, and ideation all come together. It's a fairly miraculous event. Nothing should be left to chance, and neither should this highly important stage of writing development be skipped.

Focusing a large portion of primary school English teaching on sentence creation, expansion, and cohesion helps drag us out of this modern penchant for *genre* teaching. So many high stakes tests in schools are based on asking students to write according to a genre and it actually baffles me.

Consider the fact that even in primary classrooms where excellent phonological awareness, phonics, handwriting, and spelling lessons take place, young children are asked to go straight into writing stories, recounts, reports etc. without stopping to savour the sentence. It is at the sentence level that a writer begins to hone their craft. Take your time to model, teach, and enjoy great sentences before hurtling into generating genres.

Indeed it is my very strong suspicion that children whose instruction focuses on parts of speech and syntax with a view to producing increasingly strategic sentences, are capable of mastering any genre of writing required of them. Like comprehension strategy instruction, genre instruction is only useful to a certain extent before it reaches its limit. Willingham and Lovette talk about the limits of reading comprehension strategy instruction in a piece called *Can Reading Comprehension Be Taught?* (2014), summarised thus:

"In this commentary we suggest that reading comprehension strategy instruction does not actually improve general-purpose comprehension skills. Rather, this strategy represents a bag of tricks that are useful and worth teaching, but that that are quickly learned and require minimal practice."

I dare say that pretty much similar commentary could be applied to genre instruction in writing.

DOI: 10.4324/9781003457930-13

Though I could write an entire book on the subject (and if you're reading this before *Writing for Life* comes out then please rest assured I will), we will cover the sentence in this chapter, just to give all the parts of speech somewhere to go, based on what works well at our tutoring practice and what I've learned thanks to brilliant authors like Judith Hochman, Natalie Wexler and Doug Lemov(authors of *The Writing Revolution*, 2017). I do not wish to unduly reproduce their work here, but they have helped me think clearly about sentence type and structure.

Excellent modelling, frequent practice, and deliberate development of mental models of how words behave and interact to form grammatical written statements are all essential for the development of sentence construction. This sentence writing practice should begin in the first year of school.

A quick recap

When we looked at the parts of speech, we saw that communication can take place if two bare minimum elements were present: subjects and verbs.

Nouns and pronouns function as the subject of a sentence. The be/do/have is expressed by the verb. Once this partnership is established, we have a sentence.

Sentence types

As you probably know, sentences can be categorised by type. Syntax and punctuation differ in each type. Sentence types are based on the tone they wish to communicate, such as statements, questions, imperatives, and exclamations.

Type 1: Statements/declaratives

Most sentences are like good partners in a relationship: they let you know what's happening without asking questions, telling you what to do, or bringing drama into it. These are called statements or declaratives.

They start with a capital letter, have at least one subject and one verb, and end with a full stop.

Type 2: Questions/interrogatives

Of course sometimes questions do need to be asked. In persuasive writing, there's nothing like a good question to get people to mull your ideas over.

Statement (declarative)

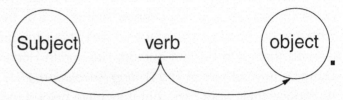

Figure 13.1 Statement example

Question sentences, or interrogatives, also start with a capital letter, have at least one subject and one verb, and end with a full stop, but the question part can be indicated in several ways. The full stop requires an extra mark above it to form a question mark, but other than that, it functions as any other full stop in terms of its constraints and conventions.

The syntactic structure of question sentences can differ from statements in a number of ways. Compare:

1) *The hen incubates her eggs.*
2) *Does the hen incubate her eggs?*
3) *Why does the hen incubate her eggs?*

1) is a statement, but can be converted into the question in 2) by adding the auxiliary verb *do* before the subject. Notice how *do* is inflected, not *incubate*.

Question 1 (interrogative with auxiliary verb)

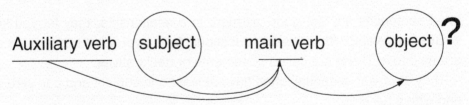

Figure 13.2 Question 1 example

3) is another question sentence, but this time adding a question word to the auxiliary verb before proceeding as normal.

Type 3: Commands/imperatives

Statements and questions are sometimes not enough. There are moments when a call to action is appropriate, and that's where imperative sentences do their duty. Hochman et al. (2017) define an imperative as a sentence that 'gives advice or instructions or expresses a request or command'.

Imperatives start with a capital letter, have at least one subject and one verb, and end with a full stop. For extra emphasis, an exclamation mark can be employed, but it is treated in exactly the same way as a full stop in terms of constraints and conventions.

Syntactically, imperatives can differ from statements by having an implied subject with the verb as the first element:

(you) Incubate those eggs!

Imperatives are used in 'how to' texts such as recipes and instructions, but with less force. They don't require an exclamation mark in those cases.

Type 4: Exclamations

The final common sentence category is the exclamation. They start with a capital letter, have at least one subject and one verb, and end with a full stop with an extra mark to indicate the force or strong emotion being conveyed.

Word selection plays a part in distinguishing an exclamation from a statement too. Exclamations can be conveyed by using advisory phrases and other command words such as the ones in italics below:

I wouldn't let that hen incubate her eggs!
We *need* to help the hen incubate her eggs!
They *should* leave the hen in peace!

The difference between imperatives and exclamations is the omission of the subject in imperative sentences.

Introducing students to these sentence types and practising their formation using a sentence type framework, as illustrated below, is a good way of developing sentence mastery. The diagram below illustrates the structure of these sentence types with a transitive verb, using our marking system.

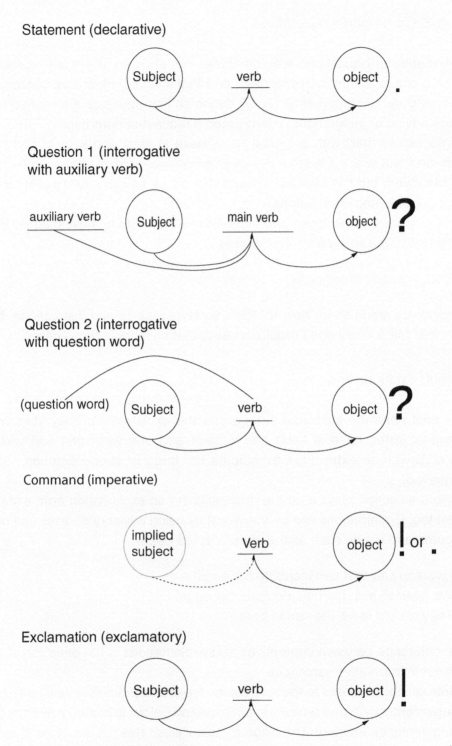

Statement (declarative)

Question 1 (interrogative with auxiliary verb)

Question 2 (interrogative with question word)

Command (imperative)

Exclamation (exclamatory)

Figure 13.3 Command example

Command (imperative)

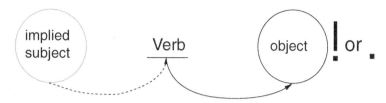

Figure 13.4 Exclamation example

Simple to complex sentences

There is also another popular way of categorising sentences by employing combinations of clauses.

Simple sentence: one subject, one verb
Example: The raven was eating.
Subject: raven
Verb: was eating

Simple sentence but a bit more jazzy: Still one subject, still one verb
Worked example: The beautiful, glossy raven was eating contentedly in its lofty nest yesterday.
Subject: raven
Verb: was eating

Exclamation (exclamatory)

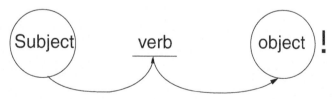

Figure 13.5 Transitive sentence types

If you want to make your sentences less simple and add even more sophistication, you can bring in clauses. These are subject/verb constructions within sentences, and can be dependent or independent. When you use dependent clauses, you have complex sentences.

Complex sentence: One independent clause + one dependent clause
The raven ate while the chicks slept.
Subject in the independent clause: the raven
Subject in the dependent clause: the chicks
Verb in the independent clause: was eating
Verb in the dependent clause: slept
Subordinating conjunction: while

You can even stick two independent clauses together to get a compound sentence. All you have to do is get two subject/verb combinations and use a coordinating conjunction, like *for, and, nor, but, or, yet, so* (FANBOYS).

Compound sentence: one independent clause + comma + one independent clause
Example: The raven was eating, but the chicks had other plans.
Independent clause 1: The raven was eating
Independent clause 2: The chicks had other plans

You could spend days on this. In fact, if you like it, I recommend you do. The important part is not so much labelling the clauses and sentences, but playing with the constituents for different effects.

The sentence type worksheet below, with a worked example, can be used multiple times with varying degrees of complexity. This will help students master the art of sentence construction. If you can build knowledge while doing this, all the better.

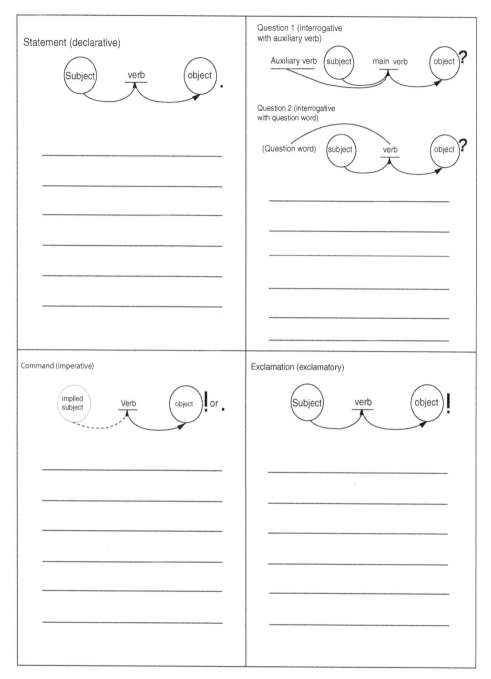

Figure 13.6 Sentence type worksheet

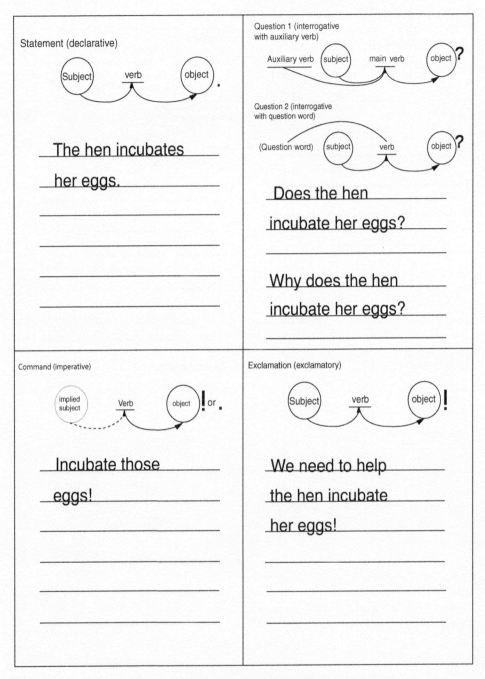

Figure 13.7 Sentence type worksheet example

14 Dictionaries

> The dictionary is an essential resource for supporting literacy learning in areas of reading, writing, spelling and word knowledge. Unlike Google, the use of dictionaries develops students' awareness of alphabetical order, word meanings, origins and structure. I find students especially enjoy working with dictionaries in my classroom and taking part in the navigation/research process for themselves. I find that when I do allow students on Google to find word definitions or to source correct spellings of words that it takes them a much greater time to do this!!
>
> I always have at least three to four different dictionaries around the class to support students' independent research.
>
> (Primary school teacher in response to online survey)

Definition

dict 'say' + ion + ary → dictionary

According to the Concise Oxford Dictionary, a dictionary is a book dealing, usually in alphabetical order, with words of a language.

By *dealing with*, we usually mean:

- defining
- pronouncing
- spelling
- working out how to use
- tracing the origins of words.

The first lesson shows how to have students learn the alphabet really well, by getting them to learn it backwards. Entries in reference materials are usually in alphabetical order so it stands to reason that alphabet knowledge is an important skill.

For most of this chapter, students will need to access a good dictionary, suitable for their grade level.

DOI: 10.4324/9781003457930-14

Webster's and Oxford offer a wide range of student dictionaries and are my personal favourites. Living in Australia necessitates the use of the Macquarie dictionary as well.

Dictionaries are incredibly useful tools if they're explicitly taught. Though many see dictionaries as a mere tool for looking up a definition or a correct letter sequence, the real truth is that dictionaries are there to showcase multiple facets of these things called words. Dictionaries will show you word class, pronunciation, usage, etymology, and, if you've got a good one, the major affixes of the language too.

Learning how to use a dictionary is not only a highly useful step towards increasing spelling ability, vocabulary, and grammatical skill, but also fosters independence and builds a student's ability to use reference materials well.

In this digital era, where the surface of anything can be summoned by a simple search, knowing how to use a dictionary is a true gift of depth.

Are paper dictionaries obsolete?

With sophisticated search engines and online dictionaries in our lives, there are certainly grounds for arguments in the affirmative.

My conclusion is twofold:

- At the time of writing, paper dictionaries were still very much present in classrooms.
- Both online and paper dictionaries are organised in the same basic way.

Therefore, learning the parts of a dictionary, and how to use reference materials in general, is still a valuable skill. Furthermore, a large majority of the teachers surveyed at my workshops over the past several years admit to not knowing the full extent of the information provided and conventions used by dictionaries. Their feedback is always positive in this regard, and they often report a renewed keenness to help their students get the most out of dictionaries.

Before embarking on the actual dictionary activities in this chapter, it's a good idea to ensure that your students can recite the alphabet forwards first. We can fall into the trap of assuming that students know this, but when I survey the children at my practice, I often find that many of them only have partial knowledge of the alphabet. Below is a summary of common findings in children above the age of eight:

- Some children simply cannot say the alphabet fluently.
- Some children skip letters or make errors in their order.

- When some children recite the alphabet, they merge the letters l, m, n, o and p to form one large word, something like: 'ell-a-menno-pee'.
- When some children recite the alphabet they insert the word *and* between the letters y and z.
- Some children can only say the alphabet by singing *The Alphabet Song* and are lost when asked to say the letters individually without the tune. Their alphabet is stored as one continuous string of sounds.

This partial knowledge has very little usefulness in the real world. The activities below are a good lead-in to the actual dictionary use activities that follow.

Teaching notes

Dictionaries vary greatly in their representation of pronunciation. Some opt for very simple notation using only the letters of the alphabet:

coelacanth /see-luh-canth/

Some adopt a relatively simple notation system using a limited set of phonetic symbols:

coelacanth /sē-lə-kanth/

Some stick to the International Phonetic Alphabet:

coelacanth /ˈsiː.lə.kænθ/

Be sure to consult your pronunciation guide and become familiar with its conventions.

Online dictionaries are a huge advantage when it comes to pronunciation. Most of them have an icon that you can press to hear the word as it is said. Paper dictionaries require a bit of prior study to get the most out of their pronunciation guides.

Many of the activities on the worksheet can be done orally. They can also be done as a whole class or in smaller groups. Make time to check back on what the groups have concluded. Try to offer a variety of dictionaries so that students can get a real feel for the different conventions across editions.

Even dictionaries don't agree, so why should we?

When working through the dictionary activities in the book, you and your students will find a slight difference in classification, pronunciation, usage, and definition of words from dictionary to dictionary. The point is, even dictionaries don't agree.

In the Concise Oxford Dictionary the word *lounge* is defined as a verb, three nouns to do with the sense of a sitting room, and one noun as an act of lounging.

The Webster's Pocket Dictionary gives it three verb and noun definitions apiece.

Australia's Macquarie Dictionary Online has three senses of the verb and a whopping seven noun entries. The Australians have really taken to the word, giving it all kinds of uses. It shares the *sofa/couch* definition with the Webster's, but only the Australians have managed to bring their love of lounges into a corruption of the French *chaise longue* with the very endearing *chaise lounge*. The Macquarie peevishly states: '**Usage:** Although deprecated by some, the form *chaise lounge* has now achieved equal currency with *chaise longue* in Australian data.' Bless them.

The point here is that, like our students and colleagues, even grand institutions do not agree on word usage. Some, like our students and colleagues, regard themselves as something of an authority above all others (the Concise Oxford Tenth Edition states on its cover that it is 'The foremost authority on current English'). Why would we expect our students and colleagues to act any differently?

Encourage and enjoy the arguments.

Resources

- Copy and laminate as many alphabet backwards cards as needed.
- Students work in pairs or threes. Each team needs to have a good paper dictionary on hand. There can be several different editions in one classroom.

Worksheet solutions

Variants

1 Look up the word *scone* and see if your dictionary gives two pronunciations.
2 If it does, which one is first?

Scone rhyming with *John* is usually given as the first pronunciation. *Scone* rhyming with *bone* is less common.

4 Look up and find the spelling variants for the following words.

centre	center
labour	labor
paediatrician	pediatrician

Syllables

How many syllables in *scratch*,
   1
computer
   3
and *wonderful*? 3

Labels

What labels does your dictionary give the following words?

   résumé (usually North American/Australian, British English favours *curriculum vitae*)
   thou (archaic)
   minor (after the first few definitions, there is also a musical label)

Usage

Find the plurals of these words.

nucleus	nuclei
curriculum	curricula but now also curriculums
salmon	salmon
graffito	graffiti
datum	data
vertex	vertices

Nouns that are always in plural form:

   bellows, clothes, contents, firearms, gallows, goggles, goods, measles, oats, outskirts, pampas, pincers, premises, pyjamas, remains, riches, scissors, shears, shenanigans, species, spectacles, stairs, suds, thanks, tongs, trousers, series, victuals

Activities

Activity 14.1 – The alphabet backwards

Suggested dialogue

We are going to learn all about dictionaries. But before we even look at one, we need to speed things up a little. Each one of you is going to learn the alphabet backwards.

I know this sounds hard, but it's actually quite easy if you take it step by step.

When you know how to do this, looking up words in the dictionary and other books gets much easier.

Give each student an alphabet card and have them learn the alphabet backwards one line at a time. Set your own time limits and games and rewards around this. Students love to have this skill.

This is what an alphabet card looks like:

Z	Y	X	
W	V	U	T
S	R	Q	P
O	N	M	
L	K	J	I
H	G	F	
E	D	C	B
A			

Figure 14.1 Alphabet backwards card

Activity 14.2 – The Position Game

Once the alphabet has been learned forwards and backwards by every student, you can start playing The Position Game. This consists of calling out a letter, then having students immediately call out the preceding and the following letter. This can be done as a whole-class activity and on an individual basis, though take care not to single anyone out who may still be grappling with the alphabet forwards.

Suggested dialogue

> Let's play The Position Game. Stand up and listen to the letter I call out. Tell me the letter straight before and straight after as quickly as you can.
>
> For instance, if I call out <g>, what two letters would you answer with? (F AND H)

Discovering the dictionary parts

Students can discover the various dictionary parts in pairs or groups of three. Each team should have access to a good paper dictionary.

Discuss each section individually, then do the exercises in the worksheet. It is best to do this over the course of several weeks, rather than all in one go. It is also important to give students plenty of practice in identifying and using each dictionary part.

Entries

> These are the words being looked up in the dictionary. They are entered in alphabetical order and are usually in bold letters.
>
> Some dictionaries put a number after an entry word to show that the word is a homonym. This means that there are other words spelt like this but with a different meaning. For example, the word *hail* can mean frozen raindrops or it can mean to signal or call out to someone. It looks like this in some dictionaries:
>
> hail[1]
> hail[2]

Students look up *hail* in their dictionaries and discuss how it is presented. They then do the exercises on the worksheet.

Guide words (paper dictionaries only)

> These are the words that show the first and last entry on each page. They usually sit at the top of every page. This is a quick reference to tell you whether you are on the right page when you're looking up a word.
>
> There is nothing that will make you stop using a dictionary quicker than having to scan page after page for the word you're looking for. Using the guide words will transform the way you use a dictionary.
>
> Learn to use the guide words and see how fast you can go. Of course, you have to know your alphabet really well in order to do this properly.

Students do the exercises on the worksheet.

Pronunciation

> Most dictionaries tell you how to say a word. Many dictionaries have a pronunciation key to help you figure out how the words are said.
>
> To save space and time, most dictionaries that offer a pronunciation guide will only include pronunciations of words that might be tricky to native speakers of English. Everyday words like *table, mother*, or *phone* generally won't be included in a pronunciation guide.
>
> The pronunciation of a word is usually entered in a dictionary between a pair of brackets. Most often they are slanted brackets //, but ordinary parentheses are sometimes used ( ) as well as square brackets [ ].

Variants

> If two pronunciations/spellings of a word are in general use, dictionaries will list the different ways to pronounce or spell it. These are called *variants*.
>
> An example of a variant would be the pronunciation of *farkleberry* in the Concise Oxford English dictionary. *Farkle-* is pronounced the same in all accents, but the *-berry* part can be pronounced 'berry', 'bri', or 'bəri'.

An example of a spelling variant would be the spelling of *medivac/ medevac*. This is a word made from combining the words *medical* and *evacuation*. Some use *medi + vac* while others use *med + evac*.

American and British English have a well-known set of spelling variants (color/colour, center/centre, pediatrics/paediatrics), but spellings also vary within dialects. Though often viewed as an American/British contrast, the spelling of words ending in -ise/ize is actually a British phenomenon. See Appendix 2 *The -ize have it* for a deeper explanation.

Orient students to the pronunciation guide in their dictionaries and do the worksheet exercises.

Syllables

A syllable is a single beat in a word. It is made with one impulse of the voice. Words often have two or more beats, or syllables. There are many different ways to count syllables and each dictionary has its own particular notation.

Some put spaces between the syllables in words:

be tween

Some highlight the stronger/strongest syllable (more on syllable strength shortly):

be*tween*

Some place dots between syllables:

be.tween

Some place dashes between syllables:

be-tween

Orient students to the pronunciation guide in their dictionaries and do the worksheet exercises.

Strong syllables

In a word with two or more syllables, one of the syllables is always stronger. This means we can hear it clearer and our voices when producing this syllable are often louder and higher pitched. The vowels in the weak syllables are often reduced in their clarity and sometimes appear in speech as a schwa sound.

If we didn't vary syllable strength in words, we would waste a lot of breath. Discovering the strong syllable in words is quite tricky at first, but a good dictionary will show you which one it is.

Again, the way dictionaries do this varies. Some put a vertical bar before the strong syllable:

be 'tween

Some put a vertical bar after the strong syllable:

between'

Some make the strong syllable bold:

be**tween**

Orient students to the pronunciation guide in their dictionaries and do the worksheet exercises.

Parts of speech

After six full sections, we finally come to information on what part of speech a word is.

A word can belong to several different word classes, and dictionaries usually list them according to how common they are. For instance, *junior* is most commonly used as an adjective, meaning 'of a younger age', but is also used as a noun, meaning 'a child at a junior school'.

Orient students to the parts of speech guide in their dictionaries and do the worksheet exercises.

Labels

Some words are only used in English in certain ways and don't appear in standard modern English, except in a certain context. This is where labels come in.

Dictionary labels vary, but some common categories are:

- formal: *terminate* as opposed to *end*
- informal: *show up* as opposed to *arrive*
- archaic: *fare* meaning *to travel* (we still say *farewell*)
- technical: *byte*

Dictionaries will also give geographical labels for words peculiar to a particular region. They often do this in a different font from the main font, for example:

fankle /faŋ kəl/ v. Scottish entangle

Orient students to the worksheet exercises.

Usage

Some words require use in a certain way, for instance *scissors* and *trousers* are always plural. *Mumps* sounds plural but is treated as singular.

Some verbs are irregular (*be, buy*, and *beat*). Some have irregular plurals (*children*, *crises*, and *halves*).

When this is the case, dictionaries will note this.

Orient students to the worksheet exercises.

Definitions

The definition of a word in a dictionary is an explanation of what an entry word means. Words can have more than one definition. These are numbered in order of how common each definition is, starting with the most common.

The word with the greatest number of definitions in English is the word *set*. The Oxford Online Dictionary gives it three main definitions, with thirty-three separate entries alone in the first main definition.

Etymology

Dictionaries also tell you where words come from. This is called their etymology. A word's etymology is like a family history and can tell you all kinds of interesting stories about a word and its relatives.

The last section of information about a word in a dictionary is usually the etymology.

Some dictionaries go very far back in history to show all the languages the word has travelled through. Some give less detail.

Looking at the etymology gives a much bigger picture of the word and also helps to associate it with other words that you might not have known belong in the word's family.

There are whole dictionaries dedicated to etymology alone. There is an incredibly helpful resource called the Online Etymology Dictionary (www.etymonline.com). If you are considering using Etymonline, please read the instructions carefully to get the most out of the resource.

Dictionary worksheet

Entries

1 Point out three entry words to your partner.
2 How does your dictionary show entry words?

_____

3 What is the first entry word on page 100 of your dictionary?

_____

Guide words

1 Point out four guide words to your partner.
2 Find the pages that *big, star*, and *flower* are on by using the guide words only.
3 Find the pages that the words *tall, moon*, and *tree* are on without using the guide words. Did it take you more or less time?

Pronunciation

1 Find and read through the pronunciation key in your dictionary with your partner.
2 Look up the words *enough, telephone*, and *shoe* and notice how the pronunciation key tells you to say the words.

Variants

1 Look up the word *scone* and see if your dictionary gives two pronunciations.
2 If it does, which one is first?

_____

3 Find another word with pronunciation variants and write them below, transcribed as your dictionary would.

_____

Lyn Stone (2025), *Language for Life* (2nd Ed.), Routledge

4 Look up and find the spelling variants for the following words:

centre   _____

labour   _____

paediatrician _____

Syllables

1 How does your dictionary show syllables?

_____

2 How many syllables in:

scratch   _____

computer   _____

wonderful   _____

Strong syllables

1 How does your dictionary show strong syllables?

_____

2 Look up the word *refuse*. How many entries does your dictionary have?

_____

3 Are there any differences in accent between the entries that are noted by your dictionary?

_____

Parts of speech

How many parts of speech does your dictionary say that the following words can be?

face   _____

fly   _____

house   _____

Lyn Stone (2025), *Language for Life* (2nd Ed.), Routledge

Labels

What labels does your dictionary give the following words?

    résumé
    thou
    minor

Usage

1 Find the plurals of these words:

    nucleus   _____
    curriculum   _____
    salmon   _____
    graffito   _____
    datum   _____
    vertex   _____

2 Find three more words that are always used in plural form.

Etymology

1 Read the guide to abbreviations in the etymology if there is one.
2 Find out where *consider*, *telephone*, and *spaghetti* come from, using the etymology in the dictionary.

Lyn Stone (2025), *Language for Life* (2nd Ed.), Routledge

15 Punctuation

Before embarking on these lessons, it might be prudent to understand that there are two laws when it comes to grammar, punctuation and syntax:

1 *You can be completely wrong.* For example, if you said that placing a full stop in the middle of a simple sentence is a good idea, you would be wrong. You have no recourse. You have faulty information and are operating from a perspective that will gain you no agreement in any sector of the English-speaking community.
2 *You can be in a position to argue.* There can be overlap. There is grey, ambiguity, wiggle room, call it what you like. In some instances you may be able to successfully argue your point. Punctuation is the area of language where personal style allows for all kinds of variation.

The history of punctuation

Written language wasn't always the straightforward, organised system we have today. Punctuation didn't even exist back in the days of the first writing systems.

It wasn't until the third century that people started to use strokes and points in paragraphs to aid separation.

The distribution of the Bible called out for a system that aided reading aloud, so more conventions were adopted, such as line breaks, initial capitals for nouns, and indentation.

It was the Irish in the seventh to eighth centuries who finally got everyone to put spaces between the words. This was the beginning of a very clear distinction between spoken and written forms of language. Spoken language is one uninterrupted stream of sounds and writing reflected this for a long time.

As with other aspects of language, the arrival of increasingly sophisticated printing machinery from the fifteenth century onwards hastened the need for standardisation. The evolution of punctuation over this period has particularly aroused passionate debate.

DOI: 10.4324/9781003457930-15

The approach in this book is to keep the two laws in mind. Much as Lynne Truss' bestseller *Eats, Shoots and Leaves* (2003) is hilarious, informative, and beautifully written, it is not this author's opinion that rigid adherence to one generation's punctuation peccadilloes will save society.

Definition

Punctuation can be defined as the marks we use in our writing to show how we mean to say things.

Etymology

Latin *punctus* 'a prick' (as in prickmark, just to be clear)
  The sixteen punctuation marks in these lessons are divided into four groups.

The terminators

These marks show the end of a sentence or the boundaries of a quote or a title. They are:

- the full stop or period
- ? the question mark
- ! the exclamation mark
- " " double quotation marks
- ' ' single quotation marks.

The separators

These marks show the separation of elements within a sentence. They are:

- , the comma
- ; the semicolon
- : the colon
- — the em dash (US usage. UK usage is spaced en dash)
- ( ) parentheses
- [ ] square brackets
- { } curly brackets

The joiners

These marks show how elements are joined to each other. They are:

- – the en dash
- - the hyphen

The indicators

These marks show missing parts. They are:

- . . . the ellipsis
- ' the apostrophe (contractions only)

Finally we will mention, just for further study, some other less common punctuation marks and say something about their functions.

Wherefore the 'possessive apostrophe'?

There is another use for an apostrophe but it has been deliberately omitted from these lessons. It is known in some circles as *the possessive apostrophe* and is that little mark that is added to a noun, often with the letter <s> to show ownership.

Much as I tend toward a descriptive rather than prescriptive view of language, I must assert something here that I believe is vitally important in the teaching of punctuation and on the subject of apostrophes.

In my opinion, this mark does not belong in the punctuation arena at all. It belongs to grammar, and, more specifically, to morphology. The apostrophe and the letter <s>, when added to a noun, is simply a suffix. Just like the suffixes *-ful*, *-ed* and *-ing*.

If you have read the lessons on prefixes, bases, and suffixes, you will have already heard this view. I would happily risk overstating it though, just to get the point across.

The English-speaking world need not be divided into two groups: those who can use apostrophes and those who can't. It is simply a matter of teaching. Traditional methods have confused the issue by lumping the possessive apostrophe in with the full stop and the comma. Actually there is no such thing as a punctuation mark called the possessive apostrophe. There is a suffix:

-'s

which is mostly attached to nouns and noun phrases (*each other's, anybody else's*, etc.). Not pronouns. Not verbs. This suffix means 'of'. The preposition 'of' in this instance relates to the noun following the suffix -'s, e.g.

> *The bird's nest = The nest of the bird*
> *A day of summer = A summer's day*

There is a lesson on this in Chapter 19, Suffixes. I implore you not to teach the suffix -'s in a punctuation lesson. I also implore you not to teach it as an isolated apostrophe, like the mark we use for contractions. That's where it becomes confusing. It is a suffix:

> -'s

As a footnote, there is some speculation that -'s is becoming obsolete. David Crystal himself, prolific author and basically one of Planet Earth's go-to people on matters linguistic, traces its history and concludes that what *should* be obsolete is poor teaching on the subject (Crystal, 2006). I couldn't agree more.

The idea here is to teach -'s separately from punctuation, leaving the good old apostrophe to do its original job: to show a missing letter or letters:

> cannot/can't
> it is/it's

This indication of omission, by the way, is how -'s began. There used to be a suffix -es that put nouns into the possessive case. There are remnants of this in words like *Wednesday*, a shortened form of Wodnes Day ('Woden' being the old English form of Odin, Wednesday is literally Odin's Day). The omission of the e led to the suffix being transcribed as -'s. It was a suffix back then and remains so today.

The terminators lesson

Three of the sixteen punctuation marks included here function as sentence endings and two are used to enclose speech and titles. They are called the terminators because they show the boundaries of elements in sentences. We will discuss these marks and then do some work with them.

Discuss with your students what they might be. They are:

- . the full stop or period
- ? the question mark

- ! the exclamation mark
- " " double quotation marks
- ' ' single quotation marks

Full stop

Also known as: period

This mark has been in existence since about the third century. *The Economist Style Guide* (2005) says, 'Use plenty. They keep sentences short. This helps the reader.'

It is now also becoming less common to use full stops in abbreviations. We can now write (hopefully without upsetting too many people):

8pm
I saw a UFO
Mr and Mrs Hollis

Question mark

A question mark indicates a direct question when placed at the end of a sentence. For example:

When did John leave for the train?

To clarify what a direct question is, let's contrast it with an indirect question:

He asked where the scissors were.

Discuss the distinction between these two types of question with your students.

Exclamation mark

Also known as: exclamation point

This is a mark used at the end of sentences that require emphasis. It can be used within dialogue:

'Woohoo!' shouted Sasha.

They can be used to emphasise a point:

That kind of injustice makes me furious!

The exclamation mark is regarded as belonging to a less formal register. It would not appear in legal or technical documents.

An even less formal use is to write several at once, though in conversational writing it happens frequently.

Note: Before the 1970s, there was no exclamation mark on typewriters. If people felt they really *must* use one, they were forced to type a full stop, then a backspace and an apostrophe! (See what I did there?)

Double quotation marks

Also known as: double quotes, double quotemarks, double speech marks, inverted commas.

In American English (predominantly)

1 They are used to show the beginning and end of an utterance attributed to another and repeated word for word. For example:

She said, "Has the Evian gone straight to my head?"

2 They are used to show titles:

In my opinion, "Hatful of Hollow" was the best Smiths album.

3 They are used to express irony or scepticism:

Peter's "friend" was nowhere to be seen.

When 1, 2, or 3 above need to be written but are already inside double quotation marks, single quotation marks are used.

When Fergus sang, "She said, 'I know you and you cannot dance' so seriously" I laughed.

Single quotation marks

British English tends to use single quotation marks for 1, 2, and 3 above, using double quotation marks for quotes within quotes.

It is, however, still common for people in Britain to *air-write* double quotation marks when they are being ironic.

The separators lesson

The comma, semicolon, and colon are often misused because they all can indicate a pause in a series.

Comma

Commas are used to separate words in a list:

   Imogen grew mint, parsley, and sage in her garden.

Even at the single word level, commas cause arguments. Some say that using a comma before *and* is a dreadful misuse of punctuation. Others would say it stops us from thinking the wrong thing in situations such as:

   My greatest influences are my parents, Albert Einstein and Oprah Winfrey.

You must be *some* kid.
   Using a comma before a conjunction in lists is acceptable and known as *The Oxford Comma, The Harvard Comma*, or *The Serial Comma*.
   Above the single word level, commas are used to indicate separation of clauses. Compare:

a) *Orla kissed all the boys, who were handsome.*
b) *Orla kissed all the boys who were handsome.*

With the comma, a indicates that all the boys were handsome. Without the comma, b indicates that Orla only kissed the handsome boys.
   Then, of course, there is the famous debate on where the comma, if any, should go in the following sentences:
   Is it:

   A woman without her man is nothing.

or:

   A woman, without her, man is nothing.

Is it:

Let's eat Grandma.

or:

Let's eat, Grandma.

Commas are also used after the greeting and closing comments in letters, although this is falling out of fashion in emails, not my emails, mind you, but I guess we all draw our lines somewhere.

Semicolon

This indicates a separation between independent clauses that logically follow from one another. Using a comma splice in this situation is known as a comma splice. Possible additional solutions are to add a conjunction or separate the clauses with a full stop. Of semicolons, Kurt Vonnegut famously said, 'All they do is show you've been to college.' If you must use them, are some examples:

* John was amused, he knew she only said it to entertain him.
John was amused; he knew she only said it to entertain him.
John was amused because he knew she only said it to entertain him.
John was amused. He knew she only said it to entertain him.

Colon

A colon has three main uses in writing:

1 After a word introducing a quotation:

In the words of Gob: 'We demand to be taken seriously!'

2 After a word introducing an explanation:

We want the windows open: it's hot and stuffy in here.

3 After a word introducing an example:

For example: bears, beets, Battlestar Galactica.

Colons are also used to separate hours and minutes when referring to time:

2:30

The em dash

This is a dash that takes up two character spaces, as contrasted with the shorter en dash. Their names come from the fact that originally the letter <m> was twice as long as the letter <n>.

The em dash shows extra but related information. It helps to introduce a phrase added for emphasis, definition, or explanation. It can also be used to separate clauses. For example:

Punctuation for Life—though the subject itself is complex—was easy to understand.

It is acceptable to use commas and parentheses/brackets in this way too. We have, at this point, crossed the line into personal preference territory.

Brackets, braces, and parentheses

Brackets, braces, and parentheses are used to contain words that give further explanation or which belong together in a group.

Parentheses (or brackets in the UK and Australia)

These are curved marks used to contain further thoughts or qualifying remarks. However, parentheses can be replaced by commas without changing the meaning in most cases. For example:

Marita and Liz (who are not sisters) both live in Scotland.
Marita and Liz, who are not sisters, both live in Scotland.

Brackets (or square brackets in the UK and Australia)

These are, as the name suggests, squared brackets used for editorial comments inside quotes. For example:

'Let them [the poor] eat cake.'

The words *the poor* were not originally said.

Braces (or curly brackets, also known as accolades)

These are used mostly in poetry, music, and mathematics. They are sometimes used via handwriting to group lines of words together, but rarely are
they used in printed material for this purpose.

The joiners lesson

Our smallest group contains two marks and they both look very similar.

The en dash

This is used to connect continuing or inclusive numbers:

2001–2003

They also connect elements to aid clarity:

parent–child relationship

Hyphen

A similar symbol to the en dash. However, it has slightly different usage rules.
Use a hyphen between the parts of a compound word or name:

eye-opener
Smithers-Jones

or between the syllables of a word, when spilling over into the next line:

I would go out to-
morrow night, but
I haven't
got a stitch
to wear.

The indicators lesson

The final two punctuation marks show where something is missing, either a
letter or a whole statement.

Apostrophe

Used to indicate the omission of a letter or letters from a word. When this happens, we have a contraction.

Some common contractions

Table 15.1 Contractions

not	aren't, can't, couldn't, didn't, doesn't, don't, hasn't, haven't, isn't, shouldn't, wasn't, weren't, won't, wouldn't
have	I've, you've, we've, they've
am/is/are	I'm, you're, he's, she's, it's, we're, they're, that's, who's
would/will	I'll, you'll, he'll, she'll, it'll, we'll, they'll, that'll, who'll, I'd, you'd, he'd, she'd, it'd, we'd, they'd, that'd

Ellipsis

Usually represented by three full stops, the ellipsis indicates an omission, especially of letters or words.

When quoting, ellipses are frequently used to skip from one phrase to another, omitting unnecessary words that do not interfere with the meaning. Students writing research papers or newspapers quoting speeches will often employ ellipses to avoid copying lengthy text that is not needed:

'To be . . . that is the question.'

An ellipsis can also be used to indicate a dramatic pause in speech:

'Never before . . . in the field of human conflict . . .'

An ellipsis can indicate an unfinished thought:

I just can't . . .

For extra dramatic effect, an ellipsis is often very helpful:

It's just that I . . .

Unusual punctuation marks

‽ *The interrobang*

The exclamation and question marks combined. Used to indicate strong emotion attached to a question:

Are you crazy‽

This has failed to catch on in English, although the State Library of New South Wales uses it as their logo.

¶ *The pilcrow*

This mark is used in editing to indicate separate paragraphs. The pilcrow can be seen in word-processing programs by turning on all the non-printing characters.

~ *The tilde*

This is used to show omission in a dictionary entry:

~smith, Maker of something using specific material as in black~, word~, silver~

^ *The caret (not 'carrot' as some may think)*

This is a mark made in writing or printing to show the place where something is to be inserted:

> to
> Sing me.
> ^

Figure 15.1 Caret example

& *The ampersand*

This symbol is an abbreviation for *and*. It is used widely. Its name comes from *and per se and* meaning 'the character by itself means *and*'. It's become very handy when worried about character limits on social media.

16 Morphology introduction

Morpheme definition

> minimal unit of grammatical structure
>
> (Carstairs-McCarthy, 2018)

In many approaches to morphology, morphemes are defined as *meaningful* units, but there are some problems with this definition. For instance, the prefix re- in *reserve* has very little to do with 'back' or 'again' as in the accepted definition of re-. In our analysis, many of these word parts have a common ancestor, but some have lost the semantic content once originally there. This requires us to think in a more abstract way about what some of our morphemes denote. This surface is frequently with suffixes too. In my opinion, it is sufficient to explain suffixes either in terms of their inflectional function, or in terms of the word category they denote. They are structural, and not always massively meaningful units.

Why morphology is helpful

It's pleasing indeed to see such a growing interest in morphology amongst educators. When I first started out as a practitioner, there was barely a mention of it. Now it's everywhere. People are realising that the study of morphemes delivers great benefits to students, both for spelling and for vocabulary building.

An increasing number of studies are showing the importance of morphological awareness, even in students who may find acquiring literacy a difficult task (Rastle, 2019; Cavalli et al., 2016). As a linguist, I've been lucky enough to have had some grounding in this subject so that I could share it with my students over the years. I'm so glad to say that there are resources and conventions of morphological study available now that have made my job much easier. I will talk a little about them here.

DOI: 10.4324/9781003457930-16

What follows is a guide for teachers, to prime you for the lessons on prefixes, bases, and suffixes. Just as we devised a simple system for parsing and analysing sentences, we will also now work with a simple word-structure system: a basic map that points to word parts and their denotations. To prepare for those lessons, you might want to read through the introduction to morphological conventions below and do the exercises to become familiar with this sort of approach.

Word sum

An analytic and synthetic tool for word study

Word sums show how words are built by teaching students to separate possible elements in words, such as prefixes, bases, and suffixes. The conventional approach is to isolate the elements and show their separation using a plus sign between each one. A word sum then ends with an arrow pointing to the word as it is spelled, once the components are put together. The arrow is often articulated during lessons as 'is rewritten as'.

In an analytic word sum, a complete word can be analysed as shown below.

We will use a range of words, going from simple to complex. Base elements are indicated in bold type. The age and writing ability of your students should determine which words you work with as a starting point.

Simple analytic word sums

redo can be analysed as   re + **do** → redo
undo can be analysed as   un + **do** → undo
redoing can be analysed as   re + **do** + ing → redoing
undoing can be analysed as   un + **do** + ing → undoing

We can also take elements and create words using synthetic word sums:

un + **lock** → unlock
re + **play** → replay
un + **lock** + ing → unlocking
re + **play** + ing → replaying

Advanced word sums (containing bound bases, assimilated prefixes, and suffixing conventions)

Bound bases:

> con + **struct** → construct
> in + **spect** → inspect
> un + re + con + **struct** + ed → unreconstructed

Assimilated prefixes:

> ad + **gress** + ion → aggression
> sub + **fix** → suffix
> dis + **fer** → differ

Suffixing conventions

Final Silent E omission:

> **make** + ing → making
> con + **fide** + ence → confidence
> **nave** + **ige** + ate + ion → navigation

Last 3CVC[1] + vowel suffix:

> **hap** + y → happy
> **stop** + ed → stopped
> **begin** + ing → beginning

Return of Illegal <i>:

> **fury** + ous → furious
> **hap** + y + ness → happiness
> **busy** + ness → business

---

1 CVC = consonant, vowel, consonant. For more information, please visit https://www.you tube.com/channel/UCil6hPEXDRn78WCKQuVXaDA.

Extension of -s suffix:

fish + s → fishes
watch + s → watches
party + s → parties (Return of Illegal <i> included)

Pronunciation effects where next element is <i>:

nate + ion → nation
de + **ment** + ia → dementia
sub + **spice** + ious → suspicion
mage + ic + ian → magician
rege + ion → region

Check for understanding (for teachers or to use in class once you have introduced affixes and bases)
Create an analytic word sum for the following:

instruction
suggest
exploratory
committee
commitment
flatten
flatly
amphibian
religious

Solution at the end of the chapter.

Word matrix

A visual tool to help explore word structure in sets of related words
There is an automatic word matrix maker at http://www.neilramsden.co.uk/spelling/matrix/ where you can input the elements you want to analyse and have them represented in a diagram. The thing to remember about word matrices though, is that they are only as good as the information put into them. They do not do the word formation for you, but merely format the word parts you feed them. You can have a good quality matrix like the one below:

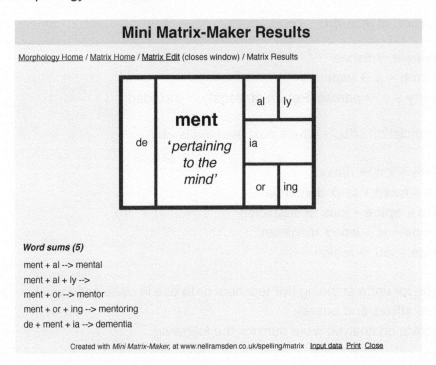

Figure 16.1 Good quality matrix

Or you can have a silly one:

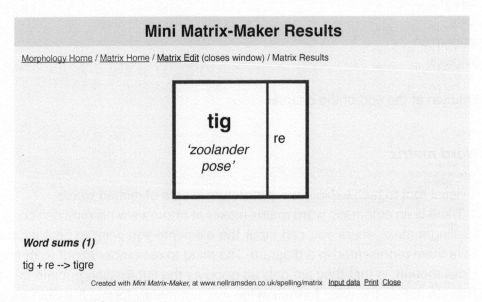

Figure 16.2 Silly matrix

The matrix maker doesn't do the thinking for you. Alternatively, you can come up with your own visuals for a matrix just by organising some word sums containing the same base element in pretty columns. It's entirely up to you.

Word Searcher

An online tool designed to help you search for elements and sequences in English words. You can input your search terms and look for a variety of sequences. The Word Searcher lists and counts them for you. This is especially useful when gathering lists of related words. Used in conjunction with Etymonline, it will save you much time and energy. It can be found at http://www.neilramsden.co.uk/spelling/searcher/.

Etymonline

This is an online etymology dictionary into which you can put searches for words and word-parts (https://www.etymonline.com). It was created by historian and journalist Douglas Harper as 'a map of the wheel-ruts of modern English.' The amount of useful information contained within this site and app is staggering. If you are going to use it, please do take the time to read the introduction and explanation; that alone is some fantastic professional development.

The diagram below is a visual guide to how the dictionary is set out. It is not in the format of a regular dictionary and isn't intended to define words, but rather to tell their stories. Studying the layout before using Etymonline is also a really good idea.

I have selected the word *morphology* and annotated the entry.

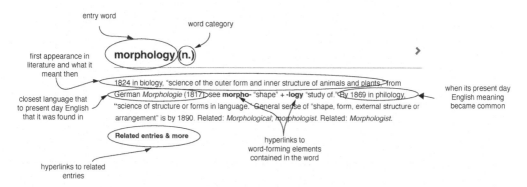

Figure 16.3 Etymonline guide

This app will not always break words down into morphemes for you. There will be times when a word's constituents are shown, as in this particular entry, but that is not its purpose. The best thing to do when breaking words down into their morphemes is to form a hypothesis and prove it with other words containing those morphemes. For instance, in the entry for the word *navigation*, you would have to be familiar with the bases nave- (ship) and ige- (move), the verb-forming suffix -ate, and the noun-forming suffix -ion. Proof of this is in the following word sums:

> nave-: **nave** + y → navy
> ige-: ex + **ige** + u + ous → exiguous
> -ate: **anim** + ate → animate

Wherever possible, the dictionary has also included Proto-Indo-European roots, which are, in themselves, fascinating and serve to bind so many words together in families with common ancestors. In the words of Douglas Harper himself: 'Originally I did not intend to include Proto-Indo-European roots, in part because there was such wide disagreement among the sources I consulted, in part because the whole field seems so speculative. But users wrote to me seeking them, so I've added them to the best of my ability . . .'

Using Etymonline

For your own practice, and for some ideas for activities with older students, there follow some simple exercises. Look up each word on Etymonline and answer the questions below. Solutions at the end of the chapter.

1 When was the first known use of *ornithology*?
2 What are the two morphemes in *ornithopter* and what do they mean?
3 What language is the closest in time to our modern version of *egg*?
4 What PIE root does *hen* go back to?
5 What other words are related to this root?

Connecting vowel letters

(Also known as connecting/connector vowels/connecting vowel letter/CVL) A one-letter structural spelling unit that connects bases to other bases, bases to suffixes, or suffixes to other suffixes.

The <o> joining vowel indicates words of Greek origin. Latin origin words can have <e>, <i>, or <u> as joining vowels.

Examples:

Greek <o> (syllabic)

ped + o + meter → pedometer

therm + o + stat → thermostat

Latin <i> (syllabic)

cone + i + fer → conifer

rade + i + ate → radiate

Latin <i> (non-syllabic)

part + i +al → partial

de + lice + i + ous → delicious

Latin <e> (syllabic/non syllabic)

gas + e +ous → gaseous

aqu + e + ous → aqueous

Latin <u> (syllabic)

sense + u +ous → sensuous

tort + u + ous → tortuous

Structured Word Inquiry (SWI)

Structured word inquiry [is] literacy instruction that engages learners of all ages and abilities by *making sense* of our surprisingly logical spelling system. English spelling can only be *understood* through scientific investigation of the *interrelationship* of morphology (bases & affixes), etymology (historical influences) and phonology (grapheme-phoneme correspondences).

(Bowers, Kirby, & Deacon, 2010)

If you like morphology, I would strongly suggest you look into https://www.wordworkskingston.com/WordWorks/Home.html. There are also numerous SWI Facebook groups to help educators at all stages collaborate and learn more about this excellent approach to literacy teaching.

Word sum solutions

in + struct + ion → instruction
sub + gest → suggest
ex + plore + ate + or + y → exploratory
con + mit + ee → committee
con + mit + ment → commitment
flat + en → flatten
flat + ly → flatly
amphi + bi + an → amphibian
re + lige + ious → religious

Using Etymonline solutions

1) When was the first known use of *ornithology*? **1670s**
2) What are the two morphemes in *ornithopter* and what do they mean? **ornitho- 'bird, birds' + pter- 'feather, wing' (an ornithopter was a flying machine designed to flap its wings. It didn't take off. Boom-tish.)**
3) What language is the closest in time to our modern version of *egg*? **Old Norse**
4) What PIE root does *hen* go back to? ***kan- 'to sing'**
5) What other words are related to this root? **accent, cant (n.1), cantabile, cantata, cantatrice, canticle, chant, chanter, chanteuse, chanty, chanticleer, charm, concent,[2] descant, enchant, enchantment, incantation, incentive, oscine, precentor, recant**

---

2 concent (n.) 'harmony, concord of sounds'.

17 Prefixes

Definition

A letter or letters placed before a base to alter the base's sense.

Prefixes can sometimes change their endings to fit in better with the beginning of the bases they are attached to. These are known as *prefix variants, assimilated prefixes*, or *chameleon prefixes*.

Etymology

pre 'before' + fix 'attach' → prefix

Teaching notes

Apart from teaching their denotations, (i.e. what they *denote*, and this can vary slightly across words, which is why we don't call them *definitions*), the following lessons delve deeper and look at a set of prefixes that change according to the base they're attached to. These are called *prefix variants, assimilated prefixes*, or *chameleon prefixes*.

Prefixes can vary according to the subsequent morpheme. This is a lesser-known but highly useful aspect of the writing system that is often overlooked in primary classrooms when young children are being taught to read, to write, and, most significantly, to spell.

If a literacy teaching approach fails to account for identical consecutive letters and their morphemic basis, this will inevitably lead to problems for a number of students.

Take the word *aggressive* for example: Teachers are often trained to view that <gg> as a 'code' for the sound /g/, when in fact, the word contains the base gress-, denoting 'move', as in *regressive, progressive* etc., and the prefix ad-, denoting 'to/towards'. It's just that the sequence /dg/ is awkward to articulate, and so spoken language has done away with the first consonant

DOI: 10.4324/9781003457930-17

and written language has reflected that by making identical to the base consonant. The word sum below illustrates:

ad + gress + ive → aggressive

That's what speech to print ought to look like, but way too much money is being poured into and made out of the sale of simplistic untruths about English orthography, bypassing the very useful, transferable, comprehensible information about morphemes. Presented here is an alternative to labelling all letter sequences as 'sounds'.

In this lesson, your students have to look up the main prefix in the dictionary, write its denotation, find its variants, and select example words. They then have to look at these words and either devise a theory as to why the variants exist, or be explicitly told why the variants exist. By the end of these activities, your goal is to make sure that prefix variants are clear in their minds. The result will be students who have better frameworks for selecting letter sequences than the dull and empty 'this is a spelling choice for X sound' as if it were all equal.

These lessons are intended for students who have sufficient skills to use dictionaries and write their example words, but that's not to say that teachers who have read and understood this chapter should keep the knowledge of consecutive identical letters back from younger or less skilled students. My advice is that if your phonics training suggests teaching double letters as graphemes, you might want to skip those parts in favour of explaining to children what's really going on. I'd also advise looking for better training.

Another goal here is to have students learn to recognise these word parts so that they can grasp meaning when they can't access dictionaries. Again, this is a skill for life and broadens and deepens your students' understanding of their language.

We're assuming that the idea of prefixes is not unknown, so we won't labour over introducing the concept. The morphology scope and sequence in this book advises when and how to introduce prefixes for the first time.

When possible assimilations are listed below, the unassimilated prefixes appear first in bold.

Students should use the worksheets and their dictionaries to find and write the denotation of each prefix. This will then become a platform for discussion regarding why certain prefix variants are used.

Prefix worksheet notes

Keep these with you when you guide your students through the worksheets.

a) **a-**/an-

Denotation: not, without
a- amnesia, asymmetry
an- anaerobic, anhydrous

b) **ad**-/ac-/af-/ag-/al-/an-/ap-/ar-/as-/at-

Denotation: movement to or towards, in addition to
ad- adapt, adore
ac- accept, accelerate
af- affect, afflict
ag- aggression, aggrandise
al- allege, alleviate
an- annotate, announce
ap- approach, approximate
ar- arrest, arrive
as- ascend, associate
at- attract, attune

c) **co-**/col-/con-/com-/cor-

Denotation: with, together
co- coagulate, coalescence
col- collide, collect
con- connect, contain
com- comprise, compress
cor- corrode, correct

d) **dis-**/di-/dif-

Denotation: lack of/opposite/apart
dis- dissimilar, dissatisfy
di- digress, dimension
dif- differ, diffuse

e) **en-**/em-

Denotation: put into or on
en- enclose, envelop
em- emblem, embellish

f) **in-**/il-/im-/ir-

Denotation: not, un
in- inability, insecure
il- illegitimate, illegal
im- impossible, imperfect
ir- irresponsible, irregular

g) **in-**/il-/im

Denotation: in, into
in- intrude, inhabit
il- illuminate, illustrious
im- import, impinge

h) **ob-**/oc-/of-/op-

Denotation: against
ob- object, obstinate
oc- occipital, occur
of- offend, offer
op- oppose, oppress

i) **sub-**/suc-/suf-/sug-/sup-/sur-

Denotation: under/beneath; behind
sub- subway, submarine
suc- success, succinct
suf- suffer, suffuse
sug- suggest (that's it!)
sup- supplant, suppose
sur- surreptitious, surrogate

Activities

Activity 18.1 – Discovering assimilated prefixes

Check for understanding. If you are going to use the term *chameleon prefix* please ensure students know what a chameleon is and does in relation to changing according to its environment.

Prefixes are a letter or letters placed before a base to add extra meaning to that base. The simple re- and un- prefixes help us make new words like *redo* and *undo*. I call them 'simple' because they basically stay as re- and un- no matter what the base is like.

There is a set of prefixes, however, that change, like chameleons, according to the base they find themselves before. This makes it easier to say the prefix and the base together rapidly. The technical term for this is *prefix assimilation*. The word *assimilation* actually contains an assimilated prefix. Look:

ad + simile + ate + ion → assimilation

The \<d\> in the ad- prefix got dropped in speech and the spelling reflected that by changing it to an \<s\> to match the base.

We are going to study this set and look for possible examples of assimilation.

Conclusion

Prefixes can vary according to the beginning of the morpheme that follows.

Prefixes worksheet

1 Use your dictionary to look up the main prefixes below and write their denotation. Find their variants and write some example words.

a) a-
Denotation: _____
Examples: _____

b) ad-
Denotation: _____
Examples: _____

c) co-
Denotation: _____
Examples: _____

d) dis-
Denotation: _____
Examples: _____

e) en-
Denotation: _____
Examples: _____

f) in- ('not')
Denotation: _____
Examples: _____

g) in- ('in, into')
Denotation: _____
Examples: _____

h) ob-
Denotation: _____
Examples: _____

i) sub-
Denotation: _____
Examples: _____

Lyn Stone (2025), *Language for Life* (2nd Ed.), Routledge

2 Next is a list of all the assimilated prefixes that go with the main prefixes above. Find two more example words for each prefix. Make sure that your example words fit the denotation of the prefix.

a) a- _____
an- _____

b) ad- _____
af- _____
ag- _____
al- _____
an- _____
ap- _____
ar- _____
as- _____
at- _____

c) co- _____
col- _____
con- _____
com- _____
cor- _____
icon.jpgac- _____

d) dis- _____
di- _____
dif- _____

e) en- _____
em- _____

f) in- (not) _____
il- _____
im- _____
ir- _____

g) in- (into) _____
il- _____
im- _____

Lyn Stone (2025), *Language for Life* (2nd Ed.), Routledge

h) ob- _____

oc- _____

of- _____

op- _____

i) sub- _____

suc- _____

suf- _____

sug- _____

sup- _____

sur- _____

Lyn Stone (2025), *Language for Life* (2nd Ed.), Routledge

18 Bases

Definition

The element in word formation that carries the main meaning of the word.

Teaching notes

The English of the Middle Ages was a language very different from the English we speak today. The entrance of Latin and Greek bases to English around this time hugely expanded the English vocabulary. Medicine, botany, literature, philosophy and law, to name but a few fields, were and still are strongly influenced by these bases.

Some Latin and ancient Greek words and word parts (morphemes) have come through French and other Romance languages (e.g. Spanish, Portuguese, Italian, and Romanian) before entering English. This makes it difficult to accurately assess the extent of the language's Latin and ancient Greek influence.

Many English words derived from classical Greek did not exist in the Greek language itself, but were formed by combining Latin and Greek morphemes. These are called hybrid words and number several thousand. *Synaesthesia*, *polyglot*, and many of the words beginning with *hyper-* or ending with *-phobia* are examples of this hybridisation.

Many words in English have been formed using bases from various other languages as well as by different methods of combination. We will explore word formation in this chapter.

Bases can be further classified as being in two categories:

1 Free (or unbound) base: A base that can stand alone as an English word
2 Bound base: A base that requires an additional morpheme to exist as an English word

Morphology teaching in the primary years happily deals with free bases like *play, help*, and *swim*. These words can be altered by adding prefixes and suffixes (*playing, unhelpful*, and *swimmers*). They are just as recognisable without such affixes and can easily stand on their own.

DOI: 10.4324/9781003457930-18

The second base category, bound bases, can sometimes go unnoticed. There are fairly obvious bound bases like the popular struct- and spect- in *structure* and *spectate,* but as you'll see in the base list in this book there are many more.

The most productive advice I can give you if you're starting out on your morphology and etymology journey (and doing one without the other is like learning to swim in the absence of water) is to remember that *every word is or contains a base.* There are no complete words in English that are simply prefixes or suffixes. What you divide words into when studying them is a matter of preference, but there will always be a base.

For example, the word *happy* can be considered an alterable free base. It denotes an emotional state, and can be altered with the prefix and/or the suffixes -ness, -er, -ly, etc. Should you have the opportunity to look further into it, you would also be well within your rights to declare that *happy* can be further divided into the bound base hap- and the adjective-forming suffix -y. Hap- recurs in *hapless*, *mishap*, and *happen*, and it denotes 'chance, luck, fortune, fate'. If you are struggling to find a word's base then there is no shame in declaring that the complete word is the base. A wise friend once wrote to me, 'Grammarians would agree that, at least in principle, morphological analysis should ignore information that's only available to historians.'

Some words look like they may contain a base and an affix, but on closer inspection are single bases. They are what's known as *polysyllabic monomorphs*. For example, the -er in *tiger* resembles the suffix -er denoting 'one who does' or 'more', but is a tiger 'one who tiges'? Is a tiger more 'tige' than something? This is where isolating prefixes and suffixes and seeing if there is actually a base comes in very handy. In the table below, I've listed some polysyllabic monomorphs. Many of them fall into certain categories, such as animals, food, and loanwords. There are many more, and it's a nice exercise to discover them with your students.

ANIMALS	FOOD	LOANWORDS	MISC
rabbit	orange	Inuit	paper
axolotl	lettuce	atrium	hunger

ANIMALS	FOOD	LOANWORDS	MISC
tiger	tomato	anorak	mascot
giraffe	mango	samovar	goblin
brolga	banana	parka	river
parrot	caramel	hoosegow	element
raven	taco	Mississippi	comet
eagle	coffee	Canada	aroma
kiwi	toffee	Bantu	molecule

There are also some bases in English called *cranberry morphemes*. They are word parts that have no other examples in English, and are remnants or *fossilised* bases. The word *cranberry* is an example (as is *farkleberry* in Chapter 14). The first morpheme, cran-, distinguishes cranberries from all other berries, such as raspberries and strawberries, but doesn't exist as a morpheme in any other English word. Here are some more:

- gormless (I'd prefer to be full of *gorm.)
- lukewarm (Not to be confused with the name *Luke*.)
- unkempt (No one is *kempt, although I'm sure plenty would like to be!)

Hybrid words from Greek and Latin morphemes

automobile, biathlon, bioluminescence, dysfunction, electrocute, hexadecimal, homosexual, liposuction, metadata, monolingual, neonate, neuroscience, neurotransmitter, quadraphonic, quadriplegia, sociology, sociopath, television, tonsillectomy

French and German morphemes were also used to form words in English. Take a look at the list of mixed-formation words and figure out where they came from using your dictionary.

List of hybrid words from a mixture of languages

around, because, disbelief, forefront, outcry, overpower, unable, aimless, dukedom, falsehood, courtship, oddments, plentiful, foolish, tallboy, travelogue, troublesome, scapegoat

A note on the term 'root word'. There are conflicting definitions in education and even linguistics about the term 'root word'. In this analysis, I will use the word 'root' to indicate an earlier version of a base that can give rise to numerous and sometimes very different bases.

For example, the PIE root *ghel-, meaning 'to shine' leads to words like *yellow*, *gold*, *chlorine*, and *gleam*.

The art of morphology relies on knowing where the boundaries are between morphemes. There is no better place to learn about this than in the study of bases.

The following activities are an overview of types of base and other interesting word-formation facts.

Bases worksheet notes

1 Underline the variable bases in the following list.

take	read
show	for
me	cry
tiger	between
dream	give
with	of

2 Look up the definition of the following bound bases, then write an example of a word that contains them.

acro-	'height, summit, tip' acrobat, acropolis
bene-	'good' benevolent, benefactor
circ-	'circle, ring' *circus, circular*
dict-	'say' *dictation, indictment*
liter -	'learning, writing, grammar' *literacy, literature*
somn-	'sleep' *insomnia, somnambulist*

3 Find the variants of these common bases and write down their denotations with examples.

fact-	'make, do' fict- fiction/fect- *infect*
fract-	'break' *fracture*, frag- *fragment*
pone-	'put' *component*, pos- *position*
sect-	'cut' *section,* seg- *segment*
rege-	'king' *regal*, roy- *royal*
cade-	'fall' *cadence*, cide- *accident*, case- *casualty*

Activities

Activity 19.1 – Variable vs invariable base words

The study of bases reveals all kinds of valuable information. For instance, did you know that there are two types of word? There are variable words, such as *house*, *run*, and *good*, and there are invariable words like *myself*, *about*, *so*, and *whether*.

Invariable words are not able to be changed. We can't add prefixes or suffixes to them. With a noun like *house*, how can we vary it? (HOUSES, HOUSING, HOUSED)

How about *run*? (RUNNING, RUNNER, RUNNING)

And *good*? (GOODNESS, GOODS)

But *myself*? (NO VARIANTS)

Try varying *so* or *whether*. (YOU CANNOT)

Most of our words are variable. We can often study their structure by isolating their parts. These isolated parts are called *morphemes*, from a Greek word, meaning 'form' or 'shape'. That is why the study of word parts is called *morphology*.

Activity 19.2 – Base variants

We are going to take six bases and write their denotation. We are then going to find words in their family and we are also going to find their variants, that is, their other slightly different forms.

For example, if you turn to your worksheet, our first base is fact-. This denotes 'do or make'. Write fact- with a comma and then its denotation, 'do, make'.

Some example words would be *factory* or *artefact*.

The base fact- surfaces as several other forms, including *fict-* and *fect-*. Can you think of any examples of words with these bases? Let's find some and figure out what their meanings have to do with doing or making.

Examples:

fiction
office
infect
effect

You can likewise review each base from the worksheets and base list with your students in this way, giving as much or as little guidance as required.

In Lewis Carroll's *Through the Looking Glass*, the poem *Jabberwocky* is explained by Humpty Dumpty. It contains many words never heard of before, such as *brillig*, *frumious*, and *burble*. Yet it manages to convey the sense of the story well.

The words put the reader in mind of other words, and this is deliberate, as the words are formed from already familiar morphemes.

brillig = broiling + (presumably) -ig/-ish. Humpty explains that it meant about four in the afternoon when people started broiling things for dinner.
frumious = fuming + furious
burble = bubble + gurgle

Lewis Carroll invented a term for this type of word formation: *portmanteau words*. Portmanteau is French for cloak-carrier. It was a kind of case consisting of two halves joined by a hinge. His intention was to express a word that carried more than one meaning.

See if you can figure out which two words are merged to form these words.

Portmanteau words

biopic, blog, brunch, carjack, chocoholic, chuckle, Chunnel, dandle, Ebonics, emoticon, Eurasia, fantabulous, fanzine, jeggings, labradoodle, manbag, Microsoft, mocktail, moped, motel, Oxbridge, Pastafarian, religulous, smog, surfactant, tangelo

Base words worksheet

1 Underline the variable base words in the following list.

take	read
show	for
me	cry
tiger	between
dream	give
with	of

2 Look up the definition of the following bound bases, then write an example of a word that contains them.

acro-

bene-

circ-

dict-

liter-

somn-

Lyn Stone (2025), *Language for Life* (2nd Ed.), Routledge

3 Find the variants of these common bases and write down their meanings
   with examples.

_____

fact-
_____

fract-
_____

pone-
_____

sect-
_____

rege-
_____

cade-
_____

Lyn Stone (2025), *Language for Life* (2nd Ed.), Routledge

19 Suffixes

Definition

A letter or letters placed after a base with the purpose of changing the base's sense or grammatical structure.

Etymology

sub + fix → suffix (note the assimilated prefix here)

Teacher notes

Once again, as in the chapter on prefixes, we are assuming that the basic concept of affixes is known to students. These lessons, then, are about the grammatical function of suffixes. Knowledge of the parts of speech is essential for this lesson. The activities below are not scripted as they were in the parts of speech chapters. Instead they consist of teaching notes to help you guide your students through the worksheets. Read them prior to planning a lesson around each activity.

Suffix worksheet notes

1 Write examples for the eight inflectional suffixes.

Table 19.1 Inflectional suffixes key

Part of speech	Suffix	Example
NOUN	-s	dogs
	-'s	dog's
VERB	-ed	skipped

(Continued)

DOI: 10.4324/9781003457930-19

Table 19.1 (Continued)

Part of speech	Suffix	Example
	-s	jumps
	-ing	singing
	-en	enlighten
Adjective	-er	taller
	-est	highest

The following words in capitals, when combined with the words in lower case, all need to be put into the possessive case using the inflectional suffix 's. For example, DOG + fleas = dog's fleas.

Don't forget to follow the process.

1	DOG	fleas	dog's fleas
2	HORSE	oats	horse's oats
3	CHILDREN	playground	children's playground
4	WOMEN	club	women's club
5	BOSSES	secretaries	bosses' secretaries
6	MICE	nest	mice's nest
7	ELEPHANT	memory	elephant's memory
8	TREE	leaves	tree's leaves
9	HOUSES	chimneys	houses' chimneys
10	CHRIS	motorbike	Chris's motorbike

Activities

Activity 20.1 – Suffix types

Discuss the suffix types below with your students and assist them by drawing the relevant word sums.

There are two types of suffix:

1 Those which tell you about number, tense, and agreement (inflectional suffixes). Word sum: in + flect (bend) + ion + al → inflectional
2 Those which tell you what part of speech a word is or which change the part of speech (derivational suffixes). Word sum: de + rive ('stream') + ate + ion + al → derivational.

Type 1: Inflectional suffixes

To inflect is to bend according to grammatical function (e.g. number, person or tense, case, or comparison).

Inflectional suffixes:

• add only grammatical information
• never change the part of speech.

Remember: If an inflectional suffix occurs, it will always be the last suffix of any type in the word.

If you've ever had trouble using apostrophes, this might just be the lesson where things become much clearer on that front. There is an inflectional suffix known as -'s. We will come to that shortly.

Inflectional suffixes add a little meaning to a base. They never change the part of speech a word is, but each part of speech has its own special set of inflectional suffixes.

English has only eight inflectional suffixes. In the worksheet, there are some examples of words ending in these suffixes.

Take your students through each inflectional suffix with the correct pace. There really doesn't need to be a lot of time spent labouring the point about grammatical constructs they mastered in oral language since they were about two years old. Number is one of them. There are some spelling and unusual conventions attached to indicating number through suffixes which you can make a decision about teaching or not teaching, depending on who you have in front of you.

Number:

> *dog* + the inflectional suffix -s → *dogs*
>
> *grass* + the inflectional suffix -s → *grasses* (the additional <e> reflects the additional reduced vowel used to separate the final /s/ phoneme from the phoneme expressed by the suffix)
>
> *cactus* + the inflectional suffix -i = *cacti*, though the habit of changing -us to -i is falling out of use. When I informally survey teachers during training sessions, a decreasing number changes -us to -i, preferring to regularise -us to -uses. Those who still cling to -us to -i also tend to vote for *platypi*, even though there is no Latin equivalent.

Person:

eat + -s = third person singular

First person singular verb I *eat* oatmeal. Third person singular verb The eagle *eats* snakes.

Tense

Verbs have three main tense-marking suffixes: -ed, -s, -ing. The main function of these suffixes is to distinguish the tense of the verb.

> verb + -ed = past tense, e.g. The hen *pecked* the ground.
> verb + -s = present tense third person singular, e.g. The hen *pecks* the ground.
> verb + -ing = continuous tense, e.g. The hen *is pecking* the ground.
> verb + -en = past participle, e.g. The hen has *eaten* the corn.

Case:

English doesn't generally have case-marking suffixes like Latin and German do, with one exception: *possessive case*. This case is also known as 'genitive', but as Prof Dick Hudson points out, the kind of knowledge visible to historians is not as useful in a classroom as we might first think (private correspondence, 2023).

We mark possessive case by adding an apostrophe and the letter <s> to nouns:

Caroline + 's = Caroline's

The noun suffix -'s denotes possession. It can be thought of as meaning 'of', as in the nest of the bird is the bird's nest.

Confusion can arise because it sounds the same as the plural suffix -s and the contraction for *is* in spoken language.

Please note that -'s is the whole suffix. This takes so much confusion out of apostrophe work. When showing possession, it is not a case of where to put an apostrophe, it is a case of simply adding the suffix to the noun; much more simple.

Confusion also comes when the noun being marked already ends in <s>. People tend to panic and do one of two things:

- Place the apostrophe before the s in the base word: The water belonging to Hastings becomes **Hasting's water*.
- Omit the apostrophe altogether: **This is James bike*.

There is a simple process for correction and teaching -'s.

1 Understand that this is a suffix containing two marks: an apostrophe and the letter <s>.
2 Determine the word that you are adding this suffix to.
3 LEAVE THE WORD ALONE and add the suffix at the very end.
4 Decide if there's an <s> too many and remove the LAST one. Example:

The plural noun, *birds*, if placed into possessive case, would be spelled **birds's*. There is no need for the final <s>, so it can be eliminated: *birds'*.

James's is pronounced /ˈdʒeɪmzəz/. If you can hear that final syllable, /ez/, then leave the apostrophe + s. This reflects the pronunciation of that word.

The surname *Connors* in possessive form is pronounced without a final /ez/. We do not say /ˈkɒnərzəz/ [FYI I have transcribed this in a rhotic accent because that's how I talk!] When adding the suffix -'s, leave the final <s> off, since it is not heard in speech: Connors'.

Use this opportunity to find more examples of <s> vs no <s> and see if you can come up with a hypothesis. In every case, it will be to do with what we do in speech.

The apostrophe used in contractions is more of a punctuation mark and should be taught as an entirely separate lesson.

Comparison

The adjective suffixes -er and -est are also considered inflectional. Traditionally they are used when comparing two things (-er, meaning more) or more than two things (-est, meaning most). The grammatical word for these forms is *comparative* and *superlative*.

> *The kiwi's egg was the bigger of the two.*
> *The wedge-tailed eagle is the largest Australian bird of prey.*

Some adjectives are not inflected by -er or -est (see Chapter 7 Adjectives for general rules concerning this). Below is a quick lists for reference.

Table 19.2 Irregular adjectives

Adjective	Comparative	Superlative
good	better	best
little	less	least
bad	worse	worst
many	more	most
far	farther	farthest
old	elder	eldest

Adjectives that don't take -er or -est:

Table 19.3 Adjectives without -er/-est

beautiful	favourite	frightening
interesting	generous	complicated
expensive	crowded	confident

You can revisit the chapter on adjectives to see where to use and not to use the comparative and superlative suffixes.

Type 2: Derivational suffixes

> To derive, is to trace the origin. In its most literal sense, words float downstream from other words through the use of derivational suffixes.

Derivational suffixes are used to indicate or derive new words. Here is an example:

entertain = verb
+ -ment → entertainment = noun

These are the four main parts of speech that derivational suffixes fall into:

- noun-forming
- adjective-forming
- verb-forming
- adverb-forming

In the example above, we call -ment a noun-forming suffix because it creates or indicates nouns. A noun-forming suffix can change verbs into nouns, as we saw. A noun-forming suffix can also turn adjectives into nouns:

loyal = adjective
+ -ty → loyalty = noun

Some quick reference tables:

Table 19.4 Noun-forming suffixes

Suffix	Examples
-hood	childhood
-ness	wellness
-ance/-ence	inheritance, independence
-ion	celebration, champion, suspicion, religion, vision
-ity	enmity, ability
-ment	enjoyment

Table 19.5 Adjective-forming suffixes

Suffix	Examples
-al	final
-ous	famous
-ish	reddish
-ent	independent
-y	muddy

Table 19.6 Verb-forming suffixes

Suffix	Examples
-ate	eliminate
-en	shorten
-ify	identify
-ise/ize	idolise/familiarize

Suffixes worksheet

1 Write examples for the eight inflectional suffixes.

Table 19.7 Inflectional suffix example table

Part of speech	Suffix	Example
NOUN	-s	
	-'s	
VERB	-ed	
	-s	
	-ing	
	-en	
Adjective	-er	
	-est	

2 Choose five noun-forming suffixes and complete the table below.

Table 19.8 Noun-forming suffixes example table

Suffix	Example
1.	
2.	
3.	
4.	
5.	

Lyn Stone (2025), *Language for Life* (2nd Ed.), Routledge

3 Choose five adjective-forming suffixes and complete the table below.

Table 19.9 Adjective-forming suffix example table

Suffix	Example
1.	
2.	
3.	
4.	
5.	

4 Choose five verb-forming suffixes and complete the table below.

Table 19.10 Verb-forming suffix example table

Suffix	Example
1.	
2.	
3.	
4.	
5.	

Lyn Stone (2025), *Language for Life* (2nd Ed.), Routledge

Apostrophe + s

The following words in capitals, when combined with the words in lower case, all need to be put into the possessive case using the inflectional suffix 's. For example, DOG + fleas = dog's fleas.

- Understand that we are dealing with a suffix containing two marks: an apostrophe and the letter <s>.
- Identify the word that you are adding this suffix to.
- LEAVE THE WORD ALONE and add the suffix at the very end.
- Decide if there's an 's' too many and remove the LAST one.

1	DOG	fleas	dog's fleas
2	HORSE	oats	
3	CHILDREN	playground	
4	WOMEN	club	
5	BOSSES	secretaries	
6	MICE	nest	
7	ELEPHANT	memory	
8	TREE	leaves	
9	HOUSES	chimneys	
10	CHRIS	motorbike	

Lyn Stone (2025), *Language for Life* (2nd Ed.), Routledge

20 Figurative language

Speaking and writing is not just a straightforward case of subject, verb, object, phrase, clause, sentence. We don't use these linguistic devices purely to comment on reality either. As we mature, we become increasingly aware of and increasingly proficient in the use of figurative language.

The great Austrian and German psychologists of the early twentieth century coined or made popular many terms that are still in use in English today. Take for example *ego, denial*, and *sibling rivalry*. There were even words which remained untranslated and one of those is *gestalt*. This is the phenomenon whereby the sum of the parts is greater than the whole.

The Kanisza figure below illustrates how a simple configuration of partial circles can create something more:

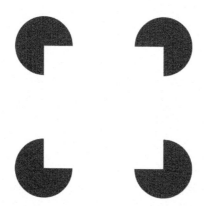

Figure 20.1 Kanisza figure

The same can be said for phrases. They may contain one, two, or more different word classes, which have certain definitions and usages on their own, but when they go together, they can function as whole parts of speech. For example:

The king parrot preens its bright red and green feathers.

DOI: 10.4324/9781003457930-20

The subject of the sentence is *the king parrot,* the verb is *preens*, and the object is the noun phrase *its bright red and green feathers*. We could take that entire phrase and replace it with *itself* or *its partner*.

Some phrases are used in a less concrete way. Consider:

My love is like a red, red rose.

The abstract concept of love is compared, using the word *like*, to a red rose. This is a device of figurative language known as a simile. There follows an explanation and some examples of common figurative uses of language in English.

Simile

As in the example above, a simile is used to endow something with the properties of another unrelated thing. Similes always use the words *like* or *as*. For example:

- tight as a tourniquet
- big as a house
- quiet as a mouse
- as happy as a clam
- sleep like a log
- as dry as a bone
- like two peas in a pod
- like watching paint dry

No text on figurative language written by me could be complete without my favourite Australian and Scottish similes:

- flat out like a lizard drinking
- mad as a cut snake
- fleein' like a clocker (*fleein'* means 'flying', in the sense of moving very fast; a clocker is a beetle and rhymes with *choker* – the whole expression means 'hyperactive')

Metaphor

meta 'over, across' + phor 'carry, bear' → metaphor

Metaphors are similar to similes, but without the use of *like* and *as*. Without these assistant words, they are slightly more abstract. Metaphors include:

- the night is young
- my heart sings
- time is money
- a blanket of snow
- a heart of stone
- a moral compass

A wonderfully amusing, but almost never deliberate, mistake in writing is to mix metaphors:

- to bite the hand that rocks the cradle
- to put all your chickens in one basket
- it's no skin off my teeth
- the spark that lit the camel's back
- it's not rocket surgery

Personification

Used best in narratives (and texts on teaching parts of speech!) to enhance the reader's experience, personification is the bestowing of human character-istics onto otherwise non-human things, such as objects, animals, and ideas:

- the wind whispered in the trees
- the butterflies danced in the garden
- the lighting flashed angrily
- the mouse smiled at me mischievously
- the cake called to me from the fridge
- the opportunity got up and left

Hyperbole

hyper 'over, above, beyond' + bole 'throw' → hyperbole

Pronounced with the emphasis on the second syllable *per* and the final <e> making an /ɪ/ sound. When someone pronounces it with emphasis on the first syllable and no final <e>, you know that they have most likely learned the word through reading (or from hearing it from someone who has), and that is a good thing. We've all been there.

Hyperbole is used to add dramatic effect. It is a deliberate exaggeration:

- You snore louder than a freight train.
- I spent a couple of weeks there one day.
- I had to walk 15 miles to and from school in the snow, every day, uphill.
- You could have knocked me down with a feather.

Alliteration and assonance

> ad + liter 'letter, script' + ate + ion → alliteration
> ad + son 'sound' + ance

When a writer deliberately uses several words that begin with the same letter to create an effect, this is called alliteration. It is similar to assonance, where a writer will use similar-sounding syllables, but not necessarily alliterative ones. This is alliteration:

> My mother makes me mash my mini M 'n' Ms on a Monday morning.

This is assonance:

> It's not the cough that carries you off, it's the coffin they carry you off in.

Rappers in particular use assonance as well as rhyme to create their songs.

Onomatopoeia

> onomato + poe 'compose, make' + ia → onomatopoeia

Many of our modern words began as onomatopoeia. This is where the word echoes the sound:

- beep, bang, click, clang, crunch, smash, meow, but also
- whistle, whisper, whisk, whip, whirl, whack, whoosh (evoking the sound of moving air), and
- bumble bee, blimp, and cliché are also of onomatopoeic origin. Look them up if you don't believe me!

Idioms

There are phrases whose words mean one thing individually but something very different when they go together. These are known as called *idioms*. The meaning of that combination is particular to a specific language or group. For instance, literally translating *on the ball* into French will not yield the idiom as it exists in English. Here is the breakdown: *on*, a preposition, and the noun *ball*. When acting together to form the phrase *on the ball*, the sum of the parts creates an English idiom meaning 'having a good understanding of the situation'.

The English language is full of idioms. Their meaning can only be derived by looking up the entire phrase. This sometimes presents problems for non-native speakers, though that's not to say it isn't a great idea to spend some time in primary classrooms explicitly teaching idioms. The list below gives some examples, but, as I'm fond of saying, the best lists are found in books. Those can be text books on the subjects you build knowledge with, or the poems, short stories, and novels you study during English literature lessons. As you will no doubt find, figurative language is more a feature of the fiction genre, but there are some examples to be found in nonfiction too.

Some idioms:

- a piece of cake
- the apple of my eye
- a nest egg
- a chip on your shoulder
- once in a blue moon
- kick the bucket
- pull your socks up
- know the ropes

21 Language myths

There is an understandable human tendency to be prescriptive when it comes to language use. People struggle long and hard to build their lexicon and figure out how to use language so as to be understood. Having achieved this, it can be difficult to accept differences in the usage others may have. To that end, it might be useful to explore some 'language myths'. These fall into two categories:

- the somewhat arbitrary grammar rules that are broken by just about everyone, including great authors
- ideas about language in general that are, on close analysis, simply not true.

In his book *The Language Instinct*, Steven Pinker (1994) dedicates a whole chapter to what he calls the 'language mavens'. These are people, who, having mastered their own grammar to the point of irrational pride, find it diverting to comment on the perceived imperfections of everybody else's grammar.

I used to be one.

It is comforting to know, however, that I am in good company. There are thousands of reformed sticklers out there. Some even write whole books about it (Kamm, 2015).

Others cling pedantically to their ideas about how people should use their own language. This is also fine, but I no longer rank among them and I have survived.

There are many studies which show the intricate scales of formality in communicative situations. This is the field of sociolinguistics and, to some extent, psycholinguistics. Though not my major field, I am proud to say that I was once introduced as a 'psycho linguist' on a live radio show. I did not argue.

Instead, I talked about language mavens but made it clear that there is nothing wrong with teachers impressing upon their students that their linguistic output will be judged, whether they like it or not. It will be judged in the same way that their appearance, posture, gestures, and attitudes will be judged. This is what humans do and this is how humans make quick decisions about others. They may not be the right decisions, but we have to have something to go on, and language is an important social gauge.

DOI: 10.4324/9781003457930-21

Children know this intuitively anyway, and adjust their language automatically depending on who they are speaking with. Giving students tools to choose their register is an essential part of English teaching. It just doesn't have to include obliteration of the language they are already using.

The following sections have been compiled in answer to the most common questions that occur during my teacher training workshops. There are many more language myths and much to be said about them. Please see the bibliography for further reading. My purpose here is to merely plant a seed regarding the validity of all communication. It's a thing to be treasured in all its forms.

Myths about language as a whole

"Some languages are easier than others."

Studies of child-language acquisition show this to be far from the truth. Children learn whatever language they are exposed to at about the same rate.

This perception is usually held when a speaker of one language observes a language markedly different from theirs. For instance, Cantonese, Mandarin, Vietnamese, and some Korean dialects are *tonal*. This means that some words differ only in intonation, rather than vowels and consonants. In Mandarin, the words for *ask* and *kiss* differ only in that *ask* has a falling tone and *kiss* rises and falls.

A native speaker of English, a language which does not rely on tone, might perceive that these tiny differences are almost impossible to learn, and conclude that Chinese is harder to learn than a non-tonal language such as German or French.

This perception merely stems from the fact that once a language is learned, the ear and brain become attuned to that and similar languages. Some languages are definitely easier to write, especially transparent orthographies like Spanish or Finnish, where one letter generally represents one sound. English, with its wide array of loanwords, is slightly more complex and so might give rise to perceptions of the difficulty of the language as a whole.

Please don't get sucked into this myth. English grammar is relatively straightforward. It has a simple tense system and very few gender or case markers. Compared to German, which has 16 possible forms of the word *the*, depending on gender and case, English grammar is somewhat breezy.

Granted, conventions that drive letter sequences, or the *orthography*, are somewhat complex, and not transparent like the orthographies of Italian or Indonesian. So be it. Complex systems benefit from sequential, explicit instruction by knowledgeable teachers. They don't benefit from pretending they're not complex.

A specific example of this, that creates instructional casualties, is the attempt to explain all English letter sequences in words as being part of some giant 'code'. For example, the elegant, memorable Greek base pter- 'feather, wing' in *pterodactyl* is explained in systems like this as beginning with <pt>, a so-called 'spelling' of the sound /t/, and thus flying (pun intended) directly past the words it resurfaces in such as *helicopter*, *lepidoptera*, and *ornithopter*.

Teachers all over the world are literally buying into 'complex code' or 'extended code' training and resources that present the orthography as transparent. If you choose not to be one of them, and look more deeply at the structure of the words and word families you're studying, you might be pleasantly surprised.

"Non-standard dialects are lazy/defective/ungrammatical."

When conducting training sessions with teachers, we keep returning to the question of mismatch between their own dialect and that of their students. The distinction is particularly sharp in lower socio-economic districts and even sharper in areas highly populated by indigenous children or children from non-English-speaking backgrounds.

Non-standard English dialects once lessened chances of success in the wider workforce (i.e. in jobs that signalled authority or were not local to the speaker).

Nowadays, it is far more commonly understood that labeLling non-standard dialects as somehow inferior is a mistake. The famous *Ebonics* case in Oakland, California (Murray, 1998) illustrates the point well.

Ebonics is a portmanteau word, coined from combining *ebony* and *phonics*. It describes what linguists term African-American Vernacular English. After several decades of linguistic analysis, and in contrast to white American popular opinion, Ebonics was found to be an expressive language, rich in terms of usage and with strict grammatical rules.

That's not to say that speech is on big dirty free-for-all and that errors shouldn't be corrected. When I talk about all forms of communication being valid, I sometimes receive questions about whether any form of correction is appropriate. My response is that speakers all possess accents, speak in a certain dialect, and have what's called an *idiolect*. An accent is the way an individual pronounces words in a language. We all have one and it indicates our geographical region or indeed our linguistic influences (including parents, peer groups, and even media). Our dialect consists of word pronunciation, intonation, and word usage within a certain geographical region or social group. There is no right or wrong per se.

An idiolect, on the other hand, is the speech of a particular individual. This is where it gets personal. This is where errors have the potential to interfere with your communicative purpose. We communicate to achieve the purpose of getting our thoughts into the minds of others as we intended them. Accent can interfere with that, dialect can interfere with that, idiolect can interfere with that. But only in the case of idiolect does it interfere in such a way that translation may not be possible.

In the chapter on language change, I revisit this with a story about code-switching.

Redundancy

Have you ever read the paragraph making its rounds on various social media sites that goes something like this?

fi yuo cna raed tihs, yuo hvae a sgtrane mnid too. Cna yuo raed tihs? Olny smoe plepoe can. i cdnuolt blveiee taht I cluod aulaclty uesdnatrnd waht I was rdanieg. The phaonmneal pweor of the hmuan mnid, aoccdrnig to a rscheearch at Cmabrigde Uinervtisy, it dseno't mtaetr in waht oerdr the ltteres in a wrod are, the olny iproarntnt tihng is taht the frsit and lsat ltteer be in the rghit pclae. The rset can be a taotl mses and you can sitll raed it whotuit a pboerlm. Tihs is bcuseae the huamn mnid deos not raed ervey lteter by istlef, but the wrod as a wlohe. Azanmig huh? Yaeh and I awlyas tghuhot slpeling was ipmorantt! If you can raed this sahre it.

Nonsense! It is not amazing in any way. Sorry to burst any self-congratulatory bubbles that may have materialised in the process of reading this misinformed, yet wildly popular paragraph.

First, there are no confirmed studies from Cambridge University on this topic. A 2003 Edinburgh University study called *An anatomical perspective on sublexical units: The influence of the split fovea* alludes to the internal structure of words and is sometimes cited as the originator of paragraphs like the one above. It certainly does not conclude that only some people can read this kind of thing, nor does it say that spelling is not important.

If you can read it then you have an ordinary mind whose lexicon can cope with some irregularity. It follows from a phenomenon known as *redundancy*.

Redundancy is a linguistic safeguard built into speech and writing that provides a belt *and* braces so that the listener/reader has multiple chances of understanding the speaker/writer. If success of communication were reliant on only *one* signal, the chances of miscommunication would be intolerably high.

S1M1L4RLY, Y0UR M1ND 15 R34D1NG 7H15 4U70M471C4LLY W17H0U7 3V3N 7H1NK1NG 4B0U7 17.

That's because you're literate. Not because you're smart. Sorry.

Not every conversation or message takes place in ideal conditions. Sound can be diminished by all kinds of environmental factors, such as distance, background noise, or the ability of the speaker.

Writing is subject to similar interference, a fact that doctors everywhere seem to know innately. The instructions below from a consultation with my daughter's allergist is at once clear and unclear proof of the necessity of redundancy.

A parent can still usually understand a small child's utterance, even if it is ungrammatical. On bringing my third daughter home, her sister, only 23 months her senior, constantly followed me around saying 'Me hod it!' It didn't take long for me to realise that she was asking, as best she could, if she might hold her sister.

Without redundancy, children might give up learning to speak and write altogether, but this is clearly not the case. They do not have to achieve phonetic and grammatical perfection to be understood. English, and indeed all languages, has a built-in system of redundancy to aid communication.

The ability of the reader/hearer is also a factor. Studies measuring brain glucose and attention have shown that humans can listen to a speaker for an average of 10 minutes before their minds begin to wander (Hattie and Yates, 2014).

Good writers and presenters know how to exploit redundancy so that their listeners get their message. They tend not to drone on and if they do repeat information, they do so in interesting ways. It's a lesson all of us could benefit from.

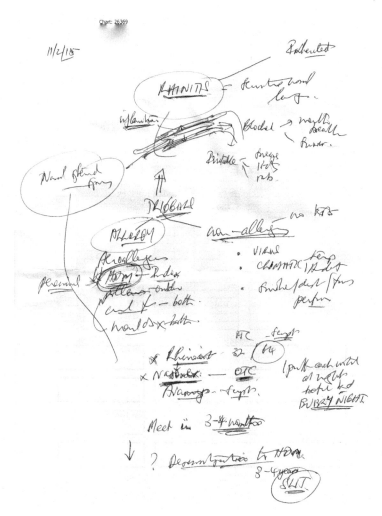

Figure 21.1 Doctor's scribble

Myths about particular points of grammar

Split infinitives

  'It is unacceptable to ever split an infinitive.'

Infinitives are the form of a verb used with the word *to*. They are a verb's basic form, e.g. *to be* is the infinitive form of *am, is, are, were*. They are called 'infinitives' because they don't express tense but rather, the general sense of the verb (in + **fine** ('end, boundary') + ite + ive → infinitive). Their place on the timeline is infinite in any direction.

In bygone years, scholars, being highly proud of the effort they had put into learning Latin, noticed that Latin infinitives were never split, and therefore concluded that neither should English ones be. Of course, this is nonsense.

A famous example of how this edict is flouted appears at the beginning of every *Star Trek* episode I've ever seen:

To boldly go . . .

I must admit, I stopped watching *Star Trek* in the eighties, so they might have changed it. But I doubt it.

Preposition preposterousness

'Prepositions are words you should never end a sentence with.'

This is another odd 'rule' that eighteenth-century Latin scholars espoused in an effort to bend English to Latin conventions.

A cursory internet search brings handfuls of snippets from the works of great authors, showing joyful disregard for such an edict. And yet there is an abiding effort to conform to this rule in speech and writing, bringing about disastrously convoluted sentences. This is best summed up by the famous retort wrongly attributed to Winston Churchill:

'*That is the type of arrant pedantry up with which I will not put.*'

It is true that informal discourse in English can put prepositions, especially the word *at*, at the end of sentences in a slightly jarring, non-standard way. Consider:

Where's your head at?
I don't know where I'm at.

There is a joke in which the following dialogue occurs:

Speaker one: Where are you at?
Speaker two: Don't end sentences with prepositions.
Speaker one: Oh, sorry . . . where are you at, bitch?

I think that sums it up rather neatly.

Sentence starts

'And for goodness sake, don't start a sentence with *and, but, however*, or any of the conjunctions.'

And why not? To be honest, if all an author's sentences begin with conjunctions, I could see how I'd want to stop reading. But, aside from the rather fragmented feel the habit gives to prose, there is actually no grammatical reason for the 'rule'.

In writing this book I was very much aware of doing this, even though I had previously avoided it. And the sense of liberty is pleasant.

I, me, myself

Is it *between you and I* or *between you and me*?

If you refer to the pronoun table in the pronouns section, you'll see both *I* and *me* there, but what is the difference? Are you supposed to knock on a door and say *It is I*? When somebody asks who the culprit is, do you say *I* or *me*?

This is a tricky pronoun, the evidence for which can be found in countless examples of child-language acquisition. My two-year-old daughter used to hide and say:

*Where's me gone? Here me are.

Tricky indeed. There is a tendency to use *I* instead of *me* in sentences with two objects:

Vicky gave Thomas and me some cake.
*Vicky gave Thomas and I some cake.

As a checking mechanism, we could take the elements *Thomas* and *me* and separate them:

Vicky gave Thomas some cake.
Vicky gave me some cake.
*Vicky gave I some cake.

In speech, however, there is much more laxity and in fact, the answer to

Who did this?
*Me!

is perfectly acceptable. We all do it.

What is also amusing is the utter distaste in some quarters for using *myself* in certain situations. In an effort to create social distance, it is quite common and certainly not a 'horrible misuse' or a 'sheer abomination' (Heffer, 2014) to say such things as

Is it just yourself tonight?
Send it to myself to sign.

Good, well, fine

Australians have done more to bust this myth than any other civilisation on the planet.

When asked how they are, the vast majority of Australians will say *Good, thanks*. Some will even go as far as to say:

Good, thanks. And yourself? (See above to get a perspective on how apo-
plectic that exchange might make a maven.)

Who/whom

If you know how to use *whom* as opposed to *who*, well done. I have some bad news for you though. It's disappearing. It's going the way of *thou* and *thine*. Sorry. Just use *who*.

Even the Oxford English Dictionary says so. I sympathise. I found it hard to let go of this one, since I was so *good* at using it. But there it is. It is likely to be obsolete in your lifetime. Move on.

22 Language change

There is a commonly held opinion in education circles that the study of language has two paths: prescriptivism and descriptivism. Prescriptivism is more resistant to language change, whereas descriptivism declines to offer an opinion on it.

In my view, this is a false contrast. Both approaches have merit and their own time and place. There is, however, a pleasing shift in education from a more prescriptive attitude to one which is inclined to be descriptive. As renowned etymologist Anatoly Liberman (2005) puts it:

> at a certain moment, the people who have no trouble distinguishing between *he* and *him* feel at a loss when it comes to *who* and *whom* and begin to say *the doctor whom we believe saved the patient*. Editors and teachers fight the trend but soon they too forget what is right and what is wrong, and the more advanced ('popular') usage takes over.

Prescriptivism

There are situations where one variety of language is championed over another. For example, a bygone standard English accent known as *Received Pronunciation* (think BBC in the '50s) was prescribed in most British schools during the 1950s regardless of wide regional variations. The section on code-switching in this chapter explores this particular phenomenon more closely.

Prescriptivism can result in some superbly illogical 'rules', such as 'never end a sentence with a preposition' or 'don't split infinitives'. The chapter on grammar myths further explores these 'rules'.

A tendency towards being overly prescriptive in teaching is often due to several basic factors:

1 Insecurity about what is correct, leading to rigid adherence to an arbitrary set of rules
2 Misplaced social superiority resulting in an urge to un-teach a perfectly good dialect and replacing it with a version of the language that the teacher finds acceptable

DOI: 10.4324/9781003457930-22

Neither method seems to result in the development of linguistically curious minds.

That is not to say that language shouldn't operate according to sets of rules. Indeed for one person to understand or accept another, the underlying rules have to be known by both. Consider the *tu/vous* distinction in French. They both mean *you*, but *tu* implies familiarity while *vous* provides social distance. Not knowing this and using the *tu* form only is considered rude.

Rules concerning word order cannot be broken without dramatically altering meaning. *The hen ate the worm* is something quite different from *The worm ate the hen*.

Far be it from any linguist to say that standardisation is necessarily a bad thing either. Before writing evolved, language structure was a matter of local convention. Grammar rules were invented to help with consistency and as an aid to understanding and are an important factor in efficient communication.

The problem is, that sometimes language conventions are prescribed without any flexibility, and this is where we run into trouble.

Just as each person fiercely guards their own idiolect, so also do they tend to guard against change in the wider dialect. A human lifespan enables the average adult to witness sometimes vast changes in the way their language is spoken and written by younger generations.

An interesting mix of resentment accompanied by delusions of superiority often go hand in hand when generations regard each other's language usage. The elders, perhaps feeling the reality of mortality, regard slang, new usages, and neologisms as sloppy, disrespectful, and unintelligent, the younger generation, in a natural state of rebellion, regard the language of their elders as overly formal, prescriptive, or just downright *lame*.

This is language change at work. Rarely is it embraced by older generations. Seldom is it curbed by the younger.

Additional to that is the inevitable personal pride of mastering one's native language(s). An infant slaves at the task for years, earnestly listening, copying, failing, being corrected, and being generally mocked. By six years old, children usually have a fine grasp of their language and spend the next 12 years or so refining it through various school lessons, listening, copying, failing, being corrected, and in many cases continuing to be mocked.

It is no wonder, then, that on reaching a certain age, a person feels justified in saying, 'I'm done. I've worked hard to acquire this language, I am a functional communicator and I'm not learning any more.' From that point on, their notion of the 'correct' structure of language begins to set and woe betide anyone who suggests change.

The myth of language deterioration

A special debate in the House of Lords in Britain in 1979 revealed an almost complete consensus that English was deteriorating. The debate was entitled 'The English language: Deterioration in usage' (UK Parliament, 1979). It is a wonderfully interesting document and can be viewed via Hansard online anytime.

Analysis of this document in the classroom would be not only a lesson in history, but also in the futility of resistance to language change.

Despite the speakers' earnest appeals to restore clarity of language to English before it presumably brought about the end of civilisation, not one effective measure was ever taken. This is because, like the march of time, it is impossible to arrest language change, no matter how you might feel about it.

Particularly amusing was the staunch anti-American sentiment that ran through the debate. Such racial prejudice is still somewhat tolerated nowadays. I am often asked, during radio interviews, to comment on the 'terrible' influence that the American language and culture is having on non-American society. It seems that being a dominant culture attracts this kind of blame/ shame attitude from the rest of the world.

As an interesting aside, the debate mentions what is now known as 'The Bullock Report'. Its lesser-known title is 'A Language for Life' (I was unaware of this report when I decided on the name for this book). In 1975 the British government launched an inquiry into the teaching of language and it was presided over by Alan Bullock. Its recommendations had profound and positive effects on teaching from that point on. It berates the practice of trying to change a child's dialect and calls it irrational, unnecessary, and inhumane. It points out that appropriateness according to the speaker's situation is far more important than some arbitrary perception of 'correctness'.

In sum it calls for a deepening and widening of teachers' understanding and acceptance of the language of their students. The point of the paper was entirely missed by the speakers in the House that day. The Bullock Report (1975) still makes compelling reading and I thoroughly recommend it.

Social media is also another hotbed of unadulterated prescriptivism. It only takes one teacher to say, 'How should I teach this word/phrase?' for a barrage of 'When it's said *correctly*, it's said like this!'

Correct for who? Who gets the label when others don't? If you're ever tempted to label some form of speech as *correct*, what do you really mean? Do you mean rich people? Do you mean elderly people? Do you mean white people? That word *correct* may be a reminder to examine your attitude for those who differ from you.

There is nothing wrong with pointing out that there is formal and informal language, but *correct*? No.

L'Académie Française

Certain members of French society (I am loath to make such a sweeping generalisation by saying 'The French') set up a rather formidable body known as 'L'Académie Française'. To get an idea of its ideological underpinnings, one only has to consider the founder, Cardinal Richelieu, and his ideas about state control.

More recently, in 1945, Philippe Pétain was removed from the Académie due to his leadership of Vichy France. He was tried and found guilty of treason in connection with his aiding the Nazi regime and suppressing the French Resistance.

The Académie's chief aim was to safeguard the French language from outside influence and keep the language 'pure'. It has been widely criticised for its excessive conservatism and its xenophobic attacks on regional alternatives to French (Basque and Catalan being two of them).

Among its self-imposed roles, the Académie tries to encourage the development and use of terms to replace 'Anglo-Saxon' influences, suggesting the replacement of *un sitcom* with *une comédie de situation* and *une banana split* with *banane Chantilly*.

As Steven Pinker remarks in *The Language Instinct* (1994), 'the purpose of the Académie Française is to amuse journalists from other countries with bitterly argued decisions that the French gaily ignore.'

This is an example of prescriptivism at its most laughable.

The two laws and why grammar wars break out

We all know what a dialect is. Dialect helps us to determine where a speaker is from. If I use the word *cannae* as in 'I cannae be bothered', you could not be reproached for thinking I came from Scotland. Similarly, if I were to say *heaps* when I meant *lots*, as in 'I love you heaps', Australia might spring to mind.

If I pronounced the word *tomato* as /təˈmeɪdeʊ/, it would probably clue most people into guessing that I originated from America.

So a dialect is a way that linguistic characteristics are shared by groups of people from a common geographical region. Those characteristics might be vocabulary (*cannae*), word usage (*heaps*), or pronunciation (/təˈmeɪdeʊ/).

Aside from our dialect, though, let us return to that little pet creature called our idiolect. This is the store of words, usages, and pronunciations particular to each individual. Our idiolect is mostly based on our dialect. Since we all have different experiences and influences in our lives, we each use language in slightly different ways.

For example, a teacher in one of my workshops was raised by an Australian mother and a Swedish father. She spoke the same Australian dialect as every-one in her home town, but, due to her father's Swedish influence, found that she couldn't help rolling her <l>s when they were sandwiched between two vowels, such as in 'holiday'. She said that word something like 'horriday'. In fact, she usually said 'vacation' so as to avoid being judged. Nobody else in the town, or indeed the family, did that. She adopted that pronunciation at a very young age and was unable to rid herself of it. That was her idiolect.

Sometimes these differences are so slight as to be undetectable. Some-times they only rise to the surface when we begin to discuss grammar. Since grammar is the way we use words, and everybody uses words slightly differ-ently, grammar discussions can quickly become very personal and passion-ate. After all, we are talking about the expression of our innermost individuality. We carry the memory of the massive effort it took to learn our native language and, satisfied with the result, we are quick to take offence at suggestions that our usage could be wrong.

This is why it is good to remember the two laws of grammar:

1 **You can be completely wrong.** For example, if you said the word *Lizzie* is a conjunction in the sentence *Lizzie plays to a full house*, you are wrong. You have no recourse. You have faulty information and are operating from a perspective that will gain you no agreement in any sector of society.
2 **You can be in a position to argue.** There can be overlap. There is grey, ambiguity, wiggle room, call it what you like. In some instances you can argue your point.

For example, if you were to say that the word *Mr* in *Mr MacMillan taught us to type* is a function word, classified as a title, you would hear firm agreement. Also acceptable is the view that titles like *Mr, Mrs, Lord, Professor*, etc. were also nouns, pronouns, or even determiners. I have a personal preference, as, I'm sure, do you, but in this case your argument would be sufficient for me to desist in trying to prove you wrong.

Number two is, of course, the most desirable outcome for your students. But as a teacher, you have to feel comfortable first. You have to be able to stand in front of a group of humans and say, 'I was taught this way and I'm teaching you this way, but I'm prepared to consider your view.' You don't have to be the stone-carved monument to prescriptive grammar that perhaps your forebears were.

All you have to remember is that grammar is a deeply personal subject that arouses strong emotions. That's fine. Go ahead and arouse them. It beats avoidance every time.

Code-switching

People are often proud of their dialect. It gives them a sense of belonging. They also have the capacity to switch out of their dialect and into a more 'standard' version of their language if they feel the occasion warrants it. My father spoke a dialect called 'Lallans'. This is his perspective.

> Working class people spoke a kind of Lallans modified by slang and immigration.
>
> Lallans comes from the English word *lowlands* and was spoken in central Scotland and the North of England. Robert Burns wrote in both Lallans and in standard English.
>
> Of course teachers were well aware that our playground language was not what they were teaching in class. They told us that we had to use standard English in class except when they were teaching Scots poetry or literature.
>
> There were misunderstandings of course, as some children found it difficult to separate the two forms of communication. One wee lad was told by his teacher to be careful with his pen in case he stained his shirt. He was baffled. She said to him, 'Don't you know what stains[1] are?'
>
> 'Aye Miss,' he replied, 'Ye chuck them.'

---

1 *Stains* rhymes with *stanes*, the Lallans word for *stones*.

However, in the main, the separation was quite easily managed. We were continually using both.

Lord Reith, the Scotsman who set up the BBC, insisted that all programmes go out in Received Pronunciation in the fifties when I was growing up that had not yet been eroded [by acceptable regional variations]. Cinema was very popular and the actors were usually from theatrical backgrounds or were American. Almost all comic strips were in standard English. Most people who did not go on to tertiary education, including my parents, reverted to dialect almost exclusively on leaving school, but they still understood standard English.

I was out of Scotland for 40 years and I have been married to an English person for 30 years. I therefore speak mainly in standard English but when spoken to in dialect, I respond in kind. To do otherwise would be rude.

Texting

Electronic communication has given rise to many new conventions in writing, including a need to abbreviate text to keep costs down. Wonderfully creative ways of saving electronic space have resulted in abbreviations such as:

u for you
gr8 for great
lol for laugh out loud (more than one person from the older generation has mistaken this to mean 'lots of love' — heaven help them if they send that in response to a message like *My cat died*.)

Some teachers report seeing these abbreviations in their students' written work, and so bemoan the evolution of this abbreviated vocabulary as another signal of civilisation's decline. My view is slightly different. Either:

- Students have not been explicitly told that they should use a more formal register, in written work, which textspeak is not. If this is the case, why haven't they been told?
- They are doing it to annoy you.

David Crystal (2008) puts it rather well in a *Guardian* article. He says of texting: 'it is merely the latest manifestation of the human ability to be linguistically creative and to adapt language to suit the demands of diverse settings.'

Descriptivism

It would be hard to find anyone who is purely descriptive in their analysis of language. As stated in the introduction to this book, I have my own prejudices, as does everybody else.

The art of teaching English language, however, is to know the difference between what you actually do and what you find acceptable.

For some, the gap between the two is very narrow. Though I'm not calling for an 'anything goes' attitude or literary anarchy, I am presenting a case for a widening of the gap.

The -ize have it

(or, is it because -ise Scottish?)

I was recently asked by a teacher why it was that I chose to use the spelling of the suffix -ize as opposed to -ise in some of the words in my books.

She was concerned that I was using 'American' spelling, and being an Australian schoolteacher, she was reluctant to use texts with 'American' spelling.

Doing a review of my endings preferences, I noticed that I used 'ize' for some words and 'ise' for others. How could this be? Is it possible I was wrong?! (This would be a good opportunity to insert an interrobang, just FYI.)

My conclusion and justification

Though in common usage in American and British spelling respectively, the -ize version of words constitutes part of a highly acceptable form of British spelling known as 'Oxford Spelling'. It is used in all Oxford University Press publications including the Oxford English Dictionary.

This seems logical to me, as about 200 -ize verbs are derived from Greek roots where the original words were spelled with the letter z. These include:

capsize, recognize, organize, standardize

As a reaction, perhaps to the prevalence of standard American spelling, some British publishing houses prefer -ise and use this ending almost exclusively. Cambridge University Press are notable agents of this.

Other words take the -ise form only:

advertise, advise, apprise, arise, circumcise, comprise, compromise, demise, despise, devise, disguise, excise, exercise, franchise, guise, improvise, incise, merchandise, revise, rise, supervise, surmise, surprise, televise

My personal opinion is that concern about this distinction in the classroom is somewhat redundant and unnecessarily prescriptive.

Children are exposed to both variants in such quantities that labouring over 'correctness' diverts attention away from striving to achieve an elegant communicative style.

Being a British citizen educated at both international and British schools, along with having lived in the United States followed by a significant period in Australia, I am unperturbed about spelling words with this distinction based on where and how I was initially exposed to them. Indeed, I have even noticed changes in my choices over the years. When a decade ago I tended towards Cambridge, I now see myself leaning more often to Oxford. There is no semantic difference between words that differ in this way, so I don't feel I'm introducing any confusion if I happen to be inconsistent.

What about 'our' versus 'or'?

Conversely, I adhere strongly to the 'our' versus 'or' distinction. I write *colour, glamour, labour*, and *favour* this way. Why don't I pick and choose my spellings according to my experience for these variants? Well I'll tell you . . .

This is a clear British/American difference, and though again, semantically, there is no distinction, I choose not to use American spelling simply because I am not American.

The *our/or* variants came about when Noah Webster was compiling his dictionary, and being a proponent of simplified spelling, he omitted the letter 'u' in words ending this way.

Other examples of this type of simplification occur in *ae/oe* forms, where Webster left out the first vowel in the digraph, such as in *pediatrics* and *esophagus*.

I have no problem with attempts to simplify spelling; in fact it's a pretty good idea within certain limits. But I chose Oxford over Webster in these matters a long time ago and now I find I cannot go back. Such is language.

Writers all over the anglophone world are constantly faced with making these choices. Some, like me, vary their choices; others are dogmatically rigid.

The important thing to keep in mind though, is to try not to be overly prescriptive according to your own personal choices.

By regularly encouraging your students to examine the language they use, and to become comfortable about noticing what constitutes a significant departure from the standard, as opposed to a difference in linguistic opinion, you stand a much better chance of raising their confidence, as well as your own.

Appendix 1 Grammar, syntax, and morphology suggested scope and sequence

How to use this document

Each year level from the foundation year to year 4 is split into a number of units of focus activities. In the first year of school, the majority of teaching time, energy, and effort needs to go into helping children develop neat handwriting and understanding the alphabet, therefore most of the first sets of activities are done orally.

Students can be introduced to the principals of sentences, i.e. subject, and what they are, do, or have, from the moment you start telling/reading them stories. It doesn't take a huge leap in logic to then convert the 'subject + be/do/have' concept into the terms 'noun + verb', and so begins grammar and syntax.

Morphology can also be introduced much earlier than commonly imagined. I recommend starting with prefixes not suffixes (e.g. -s/-es, -ed, or -ing). Suffixes are grammatically complex and require first holding a base in working memory, processing that base to the end, and then figuring out what change in the base occurs, including spelling and pronunciation, and coming to grips with the derivational/inflectional implications.

Prefixes, on the other hand, are the first element and grammatically simple, and in the case of re- and un-, require no change in spelling or pronunciation. If you want a quick, efficient introduction to morphology, re- and un- are your friends!

I have also selected the verb *do* for this purpose. 'But it's an irregular/tricky word!' I hear you say. All the more reason to practise it early. *Be*, *do*, and *have* are the most common verbs in the English language. Get onto them!

The morphemes in these units are a mere suggestion of what to cover. Many more morphemes exist, as you can see in the various lists in this book. There is nothing to stop you from using that list to expand your lessons and as a way of creating lessons as interesting words arise during the school year.

At the end of the foundation year, and at the beginning and end of every other year level, there is a check for understanding. This is a guide to what your students should know and be able to do before doing the next activities. You can use it in three ways:

- As a checklist to remind you of what needs to be covered so that you can plan accordingly
- As a 'start of the school year' checklist to make sure everyone in your class is ready to learn the next parts
- As a screener for new students or students who are in need of more intensive support

Three conditions for introducing affixes

1 When students can reliably form, transcribe, and read the letters <e, r, n, u> (amongst others),
2 When students can reliably count up to three syllables orally, and
3 When students have studied the word *do* and its family (*to* and *who* are good to study with this word, as they are high frequency and have that single <o> representing something other than the sound or name of that vowel),

you can introduce the concept of affixes.

Once the three conditions above are met, emphasis needs to be placed on students being able to form and transcribe the words or letters involved in the lessons. Teaching reading in the absence of writing is not recommended. The road to writing is far longer and littered with many more obstacles than the road to reading.

A summary of morphemes by year level

	PREFIX	BASE	SUFFIX
F	re-, un-	do, play	
1	in-, ad-, pre-, sub-, con-	struct-, -tract-, spect-	-ed, -ing, -ly, -s/es, er
2	ex-, de-, ab-, trans-, pro-, ad-, sub-	From now on, many of your prefixes and suffixes will be attached to bound bases. Rather than list them here, use your base list to find the denotation and other examples of bases that occur as you demonstrate the prefixes and suffixes.	-less, -ness, -ful
3	dis-, dia-, multi-, pan-, mis-		-hood, -y, -or, -ist, -ise/-ize, -ive, -'s
4	di-, ant-, hyper-, hypo-		-ate, -al, -ic, -th
5	micro-, mono-, poly-		-ure, -on/-ion, -ent, -en, -an
6	dem-, tele-, aut-,		-ary, -age

Suggested activities from Foundation to 3

The foundation year

FOUNDATION YEAR UNIT 1

At the beginning of every story read aloud, orient students to the fact that stories have subjects and what the subjects are, do, or have. Tell students after the story who or what the subjects were and what they did, were, or had. Play 'spot the subject/spot the verb' oral games.

FOUNDATION YEAR UNIT 2

Remind students about subjects and be/do/have but this time have students fill in the gaps 'Every story has a . . . (subject) and every subject is something, does something or . . . something' (You can vary the gaps.)

FOUNDATION YEAR UNIT 3

Once the three conditions for introducing morphology are met (see above): Write the word *do* on the board. Tell students that you can add some letters to the beginning of this word to change its meaning.
Add re-, add un-.
Discuss.

FOUNDATION YEAR UNIT 4

Revise a selection of subjects from previous stories (include people, places, things) and keep collecting more from each story.

FOUNDATION YEAR UNIT 5

Revise a selection of verbs from previous stories and keep collecting more from each story.

FOUNDATION YEAR UNIT 6

Pair your various subjects and verbs and then mix them up (e.g. *the family went on a bearhunt* crossed with *the farmer milked his cow* gives us *the family milked the cow* and *the farmer went on a bearhunt!*)

FOUNDATION YEAR UNIT 7

Remind students about *redo* and *undo* and find, explain, and dictate other examples in their reading and writing materials that use the re- and un- prefixes.

FOUNDATION YEAR UNIT 8

Formally introduce the grammar name for subjects: nouns.

FOUNDATION YEAR UNIT 9

Formally introduce the grammar name for be/do/have words: verbs.

FOUNDATION YEAR UNIT 10

Write and read out a different simple sentence every day for a week, or as the opportunity arises, and identify the subject and the verb. Point out that the subject is a noun.

FOUNDATION YEAR UNIT 11

Introduce the concept of sentences and start using this word if not already introduced.

FOUNDATION YEAR UNIT 12

Introduce the concept of capital letters for special words. Orient students to the capitals in their names, at the beginning of sentences in their readers and in storybooks.

FOUNDATION YEAR UNIT 13

Remind about capital letters and introduce the concept of full stops at the end of sentences.

FOUNDATION YEAR UNIT 14

Model simple sentences, identify capitals, nouns, verbs, and full stops.

FOUNDATION YEAR UNIT 15

Have students copy simple sentences and identify capitals, nouns, verbs, and full stops.

FOUNDATION YEAR UNIT 16

Formally introduce concept of prefixes and bases and have students identify and mark the introduced prefixes and base *do* in their reading and writing materials.

FOUNDATION YEAR UNIT 17

Provide nouns and verbs and have students select and write simple sentences and identify capitals, nouns, verbs, and full stops.

FOUNDATION YEAR UNIT 18

Once students have been introduced to the digraph /ay/, introduce the base *play* and link it with re-. Dictate and form sentences with *replay*.

FOUNDATION YEAR UNIT 19

Introduce adjectives, and model and elicit examples.

FOUNDATION YEAR UNIT 20

Revisit past noun/verb simple sentences written by students and teacher and insert adjectives by rewriting sentences with adjectives.

FOUNDATION YEAR UNIT 21

Introduce the concept of sentence type *statement* and revise conventions for statements (i.e. capital letter, noun, verb, full stop).

FOUNDATION YEAR UNIT 22

Introduce the concept of sentence type *question* and introduce conventions for questions (i.e. capital letter, noun, verb, question mark).

FOUNDATION YEAR UNIT 23

Introduce the concept of sentence type *exclamation* and introduce conventions for exclamations (i.e. capital letter, noun, verb, exclamation mark).

FOUNDATION YEAR UNIT 24

Revise and rotate sentence types using specific spelling words.

FOUNDATION YEAR UNIT 25

Add adjectives to all composed sentences from Units 21–23.

FOUNDATION YEAR UNIT 26

Dictate simple sentences from decodable reading material, students' own examples, or your own examples. Provide feedback. Check for understanding of sentence parts.

FOUNDATION YEAR UNIT 27

Introduce the concept of paragraphs containing a main idea and additional sentences.

FOUNDATION YEAR UNIT 28

Provide framework for simple paragraphs containing a topic sentence and at least two additional sentences.

FOUNDATION YEAR UNIT 29

Expand framework to contain at least two paragraphs.Provide feedback.

FOUNDATION YEAR UNIT 30

Check for understanding:
- Nouns
- Verbs
- Adjectives
- Can capitalise and place full stops at beginning and end of sentences
- Can compose simple statements, questions, and exclamations
- Definition of base
- Definition of prefix
- Can define, use and spell re- and un-
- Can define and use *do* and *play*
- Can compose simple paragraphs containing a topic sentence and at least two additional sentences

Year Level 1

YEAR LEVEL 1 UNIT 1

Check for understanding:
- Nouns
- Verbs
- Adjectives
- Can capitalise and place full stops at beginning and end of sentences
- Can compose simple statements, questions, and exclamations
- Definition of base
- Definition of prefix
- Can define, use and spell re- and un-
- Can define and use *do* and *play*
- Can compose simple paragraphs containing a topic sentence and at least two additional sentences

---

YEAR LEVEL 1 UNIT 2

Activate prior knowledge regarding nouns.
Explain noun types (common, proper, collective) and focus on toggling between them for written work.

YEAR LEVEL 1 UNIT 3

Introduce concept of determiners. Have students identify them in their own and other writing.

YEAR LEVEL 1 UNIT 4

Introduce concept of pronouns. Have students identify them in their own and other writing.

YEAR LEVEL 1 UNIT 5

Revisit sentences from Unit 2 and change nouns to pronouns or vice versa.

YEAR LEVEL 1 UNIT 6

Reactivate prior knowledge of verbs and introduce concept of present tense as contrasted with past tense. Introduce the suffix -ed.

YEAR LEVEL 1 UNIT 7

Reactivate prior knowledge of verbs and introduce concept of present tense as contrasted with future. Introduce the suffix -ing.

YEAR LEVEL 1 UNIT 8

Use sentences from Units 2–7 and toggle between past, present, and future.

YEAR LEVEL 1 UNIT 9

Introduce the concept of irregular verbs and begin gathering examples and deliberately using them in written work.

YEAR LEVEL 1 UNIT 10

Formally introduce the concept of suffixes and contrast them with prefixes.

YEAR LEVEL 1 UNIT 11

Activate prior knowledge of adjectives and introduce concept of adverbs as modifiers, specifically -ly suffix words such as *nicely, loudly, quietly*. Expand adverb work using intensifiers (e.g. *very, really, extremely*).

YEAR LEVEL 1 UNIT 12

Introduce the concept of conjunctions, specifically using *and* and *but*.

YEAR LEVEL 1 UNIT 13

Continue the concept of conjunctions, specifically using *so* and *because*.

YEAR LEVEL 1 UNIT 14

Model complex and compound sentences, and identify conjunctions.

YEAR LEVEL 1 UNIT 15

Have students copy/compose complex and compound sentences and identify conjunctions.

YEAR LEVEL 1 UNIT 16

Introduce concept of the comma as it relates to separating items in a list.

YEAR LEVEL 1 UNIT 17

Introduce concept of the comma as it relates to coming before a conjunction in a compound sentence. Revisit compound sentences and insert commas.

YEAR LEVEL 1 UNIT 18

Introduce prefix in- and show how it assimilates to bases with im- form. You can play a sorting game, where you have a card with in- and one with im-, with some bases that begin with the letters <m> or <p>, and some that don't. Students have to select which form of in- according to the base.

YEAR LEVEL 1 UNIT 19

Use sentence fragments to practise combining with conjunctions.

YEAR LEVEL 1 UNIT 20

Introduce prefix ad-, 'to, towards'.
Some ad- words: *adopt*, *adventure*, *advice*, *advent* (as in the calendar that leads towards Christmas).

YEAR LEVEL 1 UNIT 21

Introduce base struct-, 'build'.
Some possible struct words: *instruct*, *construct*

YEAR LEVEL 1 UNIT 22

Introduce prefix pre-, 'before'.
Some possible pre- words: *preorder*, *prepare*

YEAR LEVEL 1 UNIT 23

Introduce concept of altering bases, depending on which suffix is being added (contrast *sit* with *sitting* etc.).

YEAR LEVEL 1 UNIT 24

Introduce prefix sub-, 'under, less than', and base tract-, 'pull'.
Some possible sub- words: *subway*, *subtract*

YEAR LEVEL 1 UNIT 25

Introduce concept of plurals with -es. Have students identify them in their own and other writing. Do some mini whiteboard and notebook work on changing singular nouns to plurals or vice versa.

YEAR LEVEL 1 UNIT 26

Introduce concept of suffix -er and how it shows comparison or 'one who does'.
Possible words: *kinder*, *smarter*, *taller/painter*, *baker*, *teacher*

YEAR LEVEL 1 UNIT 27

Introduce base spect-, 'look, see'.
Possible words: *inspect*, *spectacular*, *spectate*

YEAR LEVEL 1 UNIT 28

Introduce prefix con-, 'together/with'.
Some possible con- words: *construct*, *combine* (note the assimilation here)

YEAR LEVEL 1 CHECK FOR UNDERSTANDING

Check for understanding:
- Noun types, determiners, pronouns
- Verbs and tense
- Simple adverbs (-ly words, *very* and synonyms)
- Conjunctions *and*, *but*, *because*, *so*
- Definition of suffix
- Definition of plural
- in-, ad-, pre-, sub-, con-
- -ed, -ing, -ly, -s/-es, -er
- struct-, tract-, spect-

Year Level 2

YEAR LEVEL 2 UNIT 1

Check for understanding:
- Noun types, determiners, pronouns
- Verbs and tense
- Simple adverbs (-ly words, *very* and synonyms)
- Conjunctions *and*, *but*, *because*, *so*
- Definition of suffix
- Definition of plural
- in-, ad-, pre-, sub-, con-
- -ed, -ing, -ly, -s/-es, -er
- struct-, tract-, spect-

YEAR LEVEL 2 UNIT 2

Activate prior knowledge regarding adding -s/-es to nouns to form plurals. Revisit irregular plurals.

YEAR LEVEL 2 UNIT 3

Activate prior knowledge of verbs and tense and show examples and non-examples of sentences where tense is consistent (e.g. *I went to the shops and I bought some bread* as opposed to **I went to the shops and I buy some bread.*) Establish this as a consistent self-check for written work and use this concept to give meaningful feedback on written work.

YEAR LEVEL 2 UNIT 4

Introduce concept of contractions and how the apostrophe is used to show missing letters. NB: Do not introduce the suffix –'s at this stage. It is confusing to have these introduced together.

YEAR LEVEL 2 UNIT 5

Introduce concept of basic word sums and matrices. Build matrices together using any previously learned affixes and bases.

YEAR LEVEL 2 UNIT 6

Activate prior knowledge of creating different words by flexing morphemes. Introduce concept of creating new words by combining bases (e.g. *motorboat, hotdog, blackbird*). Continue to build banks of compound words and use them in sentences and paragraphs.

YEAR LEVEL 2 UNIT 7

Introduce prefix ex-, 'out, out of'.
Possible ex-words: *exit, excuse, excel*

YEAR LEVEL 2 UNIT 8

Introduce con-, duct-, -ible/-able.
Contrast -ible/-able words and begin building a comparison chart containing these.

YEAR LEVEL 2 UNIT 9

Introduce concept of converting verbs to nouns using -less and -ness suffixes.

YEAR LEVEL 2 UNIT 10

Reactivate prior knowledge regarding adding suffixes like -ed and -ing to bases so thatspelling past tense verbs is accurate.

YEAR LEVEL 2 UNIT 11

Use sentences from Unit 2 and toggle between past and present tense.

YEAR LEVEL 2 UNIT 12

Introduce the concept of irregular verbs and begin gathering examples and deliberatelyusing them in written work.

YEAR LEVEL 2 UNIT 13

Activate prior knowledge of adjectives and introduce -er (*more*) and -est (*most*).

YEAR LEVEL 2 UNIT 14

Continue adjective work and introduce concept of creating adjectives byadding the suffix -ful.
Possible examples: care → careful, help → helpful, harm → harmful

YEAR LEVEL 2 UNIT 15

Introduce bi- (life) and graph- with word sums and matrices. Use this as an opportunity to show the difference between free and bound bases. From now on, many of your prefixes and suffixes will be attached to bound bases. Rather than list them here, use your base list to find the denotation and other examples of bases that occur as you demonstrate the prefixes and suffixes.

YEAR LEVEL 2 UNIT 16

Examine conjunctions *and*, *but*, *so*, and discuss the fact that they are unalterable (cannot add affixes). Find more examples of unalterable bases.

YEAR LEVEL 2 UNIT 17

Introduce the concept of function words vs. content words.

YEAR LEVEL 2 UNIT 18

Introduce prefix de-, 'down, off, away'.

YEAR LEVEL 2 UNIT 19

Introduce prefix ab-, 'away from, off, down'.

YEAR LEVEL 2 UNIT 20

Introduce prefix trans-, 'across'.

YEAR LEVEL 2 UNIT 21

Introduce prefix pro-.

YEAR LEVEL 2 UNIT 22

Introduce the concept of ad- being a chameleon (or assimilating) prefix. Use af- and ag- to demonstrate.
Possible words: *admire*, *affect*, *aggressive*

YEAR LEVEL 2 UNIT 23

Introduce the concept of sub-being a chameleon (or assimilating) prefix. Use suf-, suc-, and sup- to demonstrate.

Check for understanding:
* Irregular plurals
* Tense consistency
* Apostrophe for contractions
* Basic word sums and matrices
* Compound words
* Function vs. content words
* ex-, de-, ab-, trans-, pro-, ad-, sub-
* -less, -ness, -ful

Year Level 3

YEAR LEVEL 3 UNIT 1

Check for understanding:
- Irregular plurals
- Tense consistency
- Apostrophe for contractions
- Basic word sums and matrices
- Compound words
- Function vs. content words
- ex-, de-, ab-, trans-, pro-, ad-, sub-
- -less, -ness, -ful

YEAR LEVEL 3 UNIT 2

Activate prior knowledge regarding nouns.
Explain that dictionaries show people what part of speech a word is. Look up nouns in a dictionary and get students to observe this notation. Introduce noun-forming suffixes: -hood, -y, -or, -ist.

YEAR LEVEL 3 UNIT 3

Expand dictionary work to incorporate notation for the other parts of speech.

YEAR LEVEL 3 UNIT 4

Expand dictionary work to incorporate pronunciation guides.

YEAR LEVEL 3 UNIT 5

Expand dictionary work to incorporate usage notation, including synonyms and antonyms.

YEAR LEVEL 3 UNIT 6

Expand dictionary work to incorporate etymological guides.
Orient students to www.etymonline.com and have them begin to look into the stories of words (this can be complex in some cases, so start with simple words and do this step together).

YEAR LEVEL 3 UNIT 7

Activate prior knowledge of sentences containing subjects and verbs.

Introduce the concept of subject–verb agreement with examples and non-examples (e.g. *The flowers in the garden were beautiful* as opposed to *The flowers in the garden was beautiful.*)

Establish this as a consistent self-check for written work and use this concept to give meaningful feedback on written work.

YEAR LEVEL 3 UNIT 8

Activate prior knowledge of nouns and introduce the subcategory *abstract nouns*. Begin building word banks of these.

YEAR LEVEL 3 ONGOING WORK THROUGHOUT THE YEAR

- Introduce prefixes dis-, dia-, multi-, pan-, mis-
- -hood, -y, -or, -ist, -ise/-ize,-ive, -'s

Check for understanding:
- Dictionary parts
- Agreement
- Abstract nouns
- Possessives
- Prefixes and suffixes above

By this point, students who are well grounded in the preceding principles of grammar, syntax, and word structure need only continue to build their strategic writing skill. The basic concepts of function/content, parts of speech, altering bases, matrices, word sums, and the concepts of Latin and Greek should be known. However, it is a good idea to always check for understanding of the previous years' morphemes and parts of speech before embarking on new ones.

The more in-depth parts of speech work from the lessons in this book can now be done in the order given, using the knowledge-building paragraphs, the dragon example sentence, and the worksheets.

Appendix 2　A handy base element list

This list is a sample of base elements, compiled throughout the years using various dictionaries and in response to requests from teachers and students. Many have their roots in Proto-Indo-European (PIE) and have made their way into present-day English (PDE) through Greek and Latin. I have tried to give useful examples of words they appear in, as well as their common forms. In some cases, there is slight variation in a vowel or a consonant when these elements appear in PDE. This can be due to the word's variation in the language of origin. For instance, the Latin verb *facere*, meaning 'to do' appears as, among other things, *facio* and *feci* depending on its function in a Latin sentence. These forms give us *factory,* and *infect*

Sometimes word-parts have two common ancestors, both contributing to PDE words, such as the Latin amb-/ambi- and the ancient Greek amph-/amphi-. Both mean 'around, round about'. Both have found their way into PDE, in words such as *ambition/ambivalent* and *amphora/amphibian*.

In some cases, I have also included, in brackets, some surprising relatives found when tracing the example words back to their PIE roots. For example:

Base element	Denotation	Examples
age-, ige-, act-	do, go, move	act, action, agenda, agent, agile, agitate, agony, ambiguous, mitigate, navigate (embassy)

The three forms above, age-, ige- and act-, are all said to stem from a common ancestor (*PIE[1] ag- 'to drive, draw out or forth, move)'. The examples

---

1 From Douglas Harper, the author of the Online Etymology Dictionary: 'Originally I did not intend to include Proto-Indo-European roots, in part because there was such wide disagreement among the sources I consulted, in part because the whole field seems so speculative.

given are where those word parts are obvious, but *embassy* is a surprising one, hence the brackets.

Also, there are several base elements listed here that end with the letter <e>, even though that <e> disappears when vowel suffixes are added (see age-, ige-, act- above). This convention is common practice in word-study circles to stay consistent with the suffixing rule of doubling or not doubling final consonants. Take ige-, for example. Without the final <e>, the word *mitigate* would have to be spelled **mitiggate*. It's a fairly recent practice, generally speaking, and at first seems counterintuitive. Most approaches and dictionaries list bases as they appear in words, but I can see how it makes sense so I have included them where I see them. I may have omitted some. Understanding the writing system is always a work in progress and this list reflects my current understanding. A list this extensive will always have areas that may be updated in future lists, but it is by no means exhaustive. If I've left something off that you feel should be on it, feel free to let me know or, even better, compile your own list. Members of this list are simply word parts that I've found interesting or useful over the years.

I have not included prefixes and suffixes, therefore these word parts can be considered bases or word-forming elements. However, arguments about what does and doesn't constitute a root or a base, or a word-forming element abound in and around education, and though I've tried to be as purist as I can, I'm actually more concerned with compiling a handy list that can be taught to students to help them read, write, and understand complex words better. If you want to study Latin and ancient Greek so that you can 'attest' bases according to someone's theory or approach, be my guest. I cannot speak highly enough of the scholarship and insight that goes into this kind of study, but that is not the scope of this chapter.

But users wrote to me seeking them, so I've added them to the best of my ability, mainly based on the Watkins "American Heritage Dictionary of Indo-European Roots" but also by consulting Pokorny and such modern works as are available for Latin, Greek, and Germanic in the Leiden Indo-European Etymological Dictionary Series . . . With many words, root meanings or sense evolutions remain obscure. I would be content to leave them as such, but readers are curious to know what guesses have been made (or dismissed) by the experts, as well as what facts have been settled. So I've included such speculations that have appeared in the sources I consulted. They ought to be prefaced by "perhaps" in this text, even where the sources say "probably."'

Similarly the notation here is as you see notation in most dictionaries and the Online Etymology dictionary, in that these elements have a hyphen after them to denote that they are word-parts rather than words themselves. There is no danger of confusing them with prefixes here, as the prefix and suffix list are separate from this list.

Instead of listing the second column as 'meaning', I have used the word 'denotation', as meaning is a slippery fish. Rather, these elements denote a sense, sometimes very close to PDE usage, and sometimes more remote. Thinking about this is itself a rich and valuable exercise.

Should an element or example word intrigue you, I would encourage you to use the Online Etymology Dictionary (www.etymonline.com) to look deeper into it, so that you can plan a great lesson around it.

I also advise using a word-study framework, such as Structured Word Inquiry, synthetic and analytic word sums, word matrices, and/or my own 4-Step Process if word study is what you have in mind.

Whatever you do, I hope this list serves my intended purpose of showing how words exist in networks can can be planted much more fruitfully in the minds of students when studied alongside related words.

Base	Denotation	Examples
ac-	sharp, pointed	acid, acupuncture, acute
acro-	height, summit, tip	acrobatics, acronym, acropolis
aero-	air, atmosphere	aerobic, aerodynamic, aeronautics, aerosol
age-, ige-, act-	do, go, move	act, action, agenda, agent, agile, agitate, agony, ambiguous, mitigate, navigate (embassy)
alg-	pain	analgesic, fibromyalgia, neuralgia
ali-, alter-	other	alias, alibi, alien, alter, alternate
alti-	high, deep	altimeter, altitude
ame-	love, liking	amateur, amatory, amenity, amiable, amicable, amorous, enamoured

Base	Denotation	Examples
ambi-, amphi	both, on both sides	ambidextrous, ambient, ambiguous, ambition, ambivalent, amphibian, amphitheatre
anem-, anim-	wind, breath, life, spirit	anemometer, anemone, animal, animate
ann-, enn-	year, yearly	anniversary, annual, centennial, millennium, perennial
ant-, anti-	against, opposed to	antagonist, antagonise, antibiotic, anterior, antique
ante-, anti-	before, in front of, prior to	antediluvian, ante meridiem (a.m.), anticipate
aqu-	water	aquamarine, aquarium, aqueduct, aquifer
arch-	ruler	anarchy, archangel, archetype, architect, monarchy
archae-	ancient	archaeology, archaic, archaism
arthr-	joint	arthritic, arthritis, arthropod
aster-, astr-	star, star-shaped	aster, asterisk, asteroid, astronaut, astrology, astronomy
aud-	hearing, listening, sound	audible, audience, audio, audiology, audition, auditorium
aug-, auct-	grow, increase	auction, augment, augmentation, inauguration
aut-	self, directed from within	autism, autobiography, autocracy, autograph, automatic, autonomy
avi-	bird, egg	aviary, aviation, caviar
bal-, bole-	throw	ball, ballet, ballistic, hyperbole, metabolism
bare-	weight, pressure	barometer, hyperbaric

Base	Denotation	Examples
base-	bottom	base, basic, debase
bel-	war	bellicose, belligerent, rebellion
bene-	good, well	benefit, benevolent, benign
bi-	two	bicycle, biennial, binary, binoculars
bi-	life	amphibian, biography, biology
bibl-	book	bible, bibliography
brev-	a short time	abbreviate, brevity, (brief)
bront-	thunder	brontosaurus, brontology, brontophobia
burs-	pouch, purse	bursar, bursitis, disburse
cade-, cide-, case-	fall	accident, cadence, casualty, coincidence (chance)
calc-	chalk	calcite, calcium, calculate
camp-	field	camp, campaign, (champion)
cant-, cent-,	sing	accent, incentive, recant (hen)
cand-, cend-	shine	candle, candour, incandescent, incendiary, (incense)
cape-, cipe-, cep-, cept-	hold, take, grasp	capable, capacity, captive, concept, except, forceps, incipient, municipal (prince)
capit-, cipit-	head	cap, capital, captain, decapitate, precipitation
carn-	flesh	carnage, carnival, carnivore, reincarnation
cata-, cat-	down	catalyst, catastrophe, catatonic, cathode
caust-, caut-	burn	caustic, cauterise, holocaust

Base	Denotation	Examples
cave-	hollow	cave, cavity, excavation, concave
cens-	to assess	censure, census
cent-	hundred	cent, centennial, centurion, percent
chlore-	green	chlorine, chlorophyll, chloroplast
chore-	relating to dance	choreography, chorus, terpsichorean
chrome-	colour	chromatic, chrome, chromium, chromosome, monochrome
chrone-	time	anachronism, chronic, chronicle, chronology, chronometer, synchronise
circ-	circle, ring	circle, circular, circulate, circumference, circus
cite-	call, urge	citation, cite, excite, incite, solicit
cive-, cite-	town	civic, civil, civilian, civilisation
claud-, clud-, claus-, clus-	close, shut	clause, claustrophobia, conclude, exclude, exclusive, include, occlusion, recluse, seclude
clave-	key	clavichord, clavicle, conclave
contra-	against	contraband, contradict, contrast
cope-	plenty	copious, copy, cornucopia (interestingly, this can be traced back to the prefix com- and the PIE root *op-, 'to work, produce in abundance')
core-, card-	heart	accord, cardiac, cordial, core, concord, courage, discord, encourage
corn-	horn	cornea, cornucopia, unicorn
coron-	crown	corona, coronation
corp-, corpor-	body	corporation, corporal, corpse, incorporate

Base	Denotation	Examples
cosm-	universe	cosmic, cosmonaut, cosmopolitan, cosmos, microcosm
crede- (**related to** *heart*)	believe, trust	accreditation, credentials, credibility, credo, creed, discredit, incredible
crite-, cris-	judge, separate	crisis, criterion, critic, hypocrisy
cruci-	cross	crucial, crucify, excruciating (crux)
cryp-	hidden	apocryphal, cryptic, cryptography
culp-	blame, fault	culpable, culprit, exculpate
cure-	care for	accurate, curator, cure, curious, manicure
cur-, cor-	run, course	concur, corridor, course, currency, cursive, occur (courier)
curve-	bent	curvature, curve (curb)
cul-, col-	cultivate, till, inhabit	colony, cult, cultivate, cultivation, culture
cut-	skin	cutaneous, cuticle
cycl-	circular	bicycle, cycle, cyclic, cyclone, unicycle
damn-, demn-	to inflict loss upon	condemn, damnation, indemnify
dec-	ten	decade, decahedron, decathlon, decimal
decor-	ornament	decorate, decorous, decorum
deme-	people	democracy, demographic, endemic, epidemic
dense-	thick	condense, dense, density
dent-	tooth	dental, dentures
derm-	skin	dermatology, hypodermic, taxidermy
dextr-	on the right	ambidextrous, dexterity, dextrose

Base	Denotation	Examples
di-	two	digraph, dichotomy
dia-	through	diagram, dialysis, diameter, diarrhoea
dict-	say, speak	dictate, dictionary, dictum, edict, verdict
doct-, doc-	teach/learn	docile, doctor, doctrine, document, indoctrinate
dog-, dox-	opinion, tenet	dogma, orthodox, paradox
dole-	pain	condolence, doleful, indolence
dome-	master, household	domain, domestic, dominate, dominion, domino (dame)
done-, ded	give	condone, donate, donor, pardon (dose, dowry)
dorm-	sleep	dormant, dormitory
dors-	back	dorsal, dorsum, dossier, endorse
drom-	run	dromedary, hippodrome, palindrome, syndrome
du-	two	deuce, dual, duo, duplicity
duce-, duct-	lead	abduct, deduce (dux)
dure-	hard	duration, duress, endure
dyna-	power	dynamic, dynamite, dynamo, dynasty
eco-	house	ecology, economics
ecto-	outside	ectoderm, ectoplasm
ed-, es-	eat	edible, obesity
em-, en-	put into or on	embody, embellish, emblem, enclose, envelop, enshrine
endo-	inside, within	endocrine, endomorph

Base	Denotation	Examples
epi-	upon	epicentre, epidemic, epitaph, epiphany
equ-	even, equal, level	equate, equilibrium, equinox, inequity
erg-	work	energy, ergonomic
err-	stray	aberration, error
eu-	well, good	eugenics, euphoria, euthanasia
extra-	outer	extra, extraordinary, strange
fact-, fect-, fic-/fict-	make, do	factory, infect, difficult (malfeasance)
fal-	false, deceive	fallacy, fallible, false, (fault, fail)
famili-	a close attendant	familiar, family
fatu-	foolish, useless	fatuous, infatuation
felice-	happy, merry	felicity, felicitations
fend-, fense-	strike	defend, fence, offense
fer-	to bear, carry	circumference, confer, offer, prefer, refer, transfer, vociferous (but not ferry!)
fer-	boil, glow	ferment, fervent, fervour, (fever)
fide-	faith, trust	confidence, diffident, (faith)
file-	thread	defile, filament, file, filigree, filet, profile
fili-	son	affiliation, filial
fine-	end	definite, final, finish
fix-	attach	affix, fix, fixation, fixture, prefix, suffix
flect-, flex-	bend	deflect, flexible, inflection, reflect, reflection, reflex
flig-, flict-	strike	afflict, conflict, inflict, profligate
flore-	f lower	floral, florid, florist

Base	Denotation	Examples
flu-	flow	affluent, fluctuate, fluent, fluid, flush, influence
foli-	leaf	defoliant, exfoliate, folio
form-	shape	conform, deform, formula, uniform
fort-	strong	forte, fortify, fortitude
fract-, frag-	break	fraction, fracture, fragile, fragment, fray, infraction, infringe, refrain
fric-, frict-	rub	dentifrice, friction
frige-	cold	frigid, refrigerator
fuge-	flee	centrifuge, fugitive, refuge
fund-, found-	bottom	founder, foundation, fund, fundamental, profound
fuse-	pour	profuse, transfusion
game-	marriage, wedding	gamete, monogamy, polygamy
gamb-	leg	gam, gambit, gambol, gammon
gar-	chatter	gargle, garrulous (jargon)
gastr-	stomach	gastric, gastronomic, gastropod
geo-	earth	geography, geology, geometry
gene-	born, of a specified kind	congenial, engender, gender, generate, genital, genus, indigenous, progeny
gere-	old	geriatric, gerontology
gest-	bear, carry	congest, digest, gestation, suggest
germ-	seed	germ, germane, germinate, wheatgerm
globe-	sphere	global, globe, globule
gloss-, glot-	tongue	epiglottis, glossary, polyglot

Base	Denotation	Examples
gn-	know	agnostic, ignorant, prognosis
gon-	corner, angle, knee	polygon, trigonometry (genuflect)
grad-, gred-, gress-	walk, step, go	aggression, egress, grade, gradual, graduate, progress, regress, transgress
gram-	letter, writing	anagram, diagram, grammar, hologram, monogram, programme
grane-	grain	granary, granite, granola, granule
graph-	draw, write	autograph, digraph, graph, grapheme, graphic, orthography, paragraph, photograph
grate-	thank, please	congratulate, grace, grateful, ingratiate
grave-	heavy	aggravate, grave, gravitate, gravity
grege-	flock, herd	aggregate, congregation, gregarious, segregation
gust-	taste	degustation, disgust, gusto
gyne-, gynae-	woman	gynaecology, misogynist
habe-, hibe-	have, hold	habit, prohibition
haemo- (US hemo-)	blood	haemophilia, haemoglobin, haemorrhage
hale-	breathe	inhale, halitosis
hap-	luck, chance, fortune	hapless, happy, mishap
helio-	sun	heliocentric, heliotrope, helium
helico-	turn, spiral	helicopter, helicobacter (helix)
hemi-	half	hemicycle, hemisphere
hept-	seven	heptagon, heptathlon
here-	succession	heredity, heritage, inherit (heir)

Base	Denotation	Examples
here-, hese-	cling, stick	adhere, adhesive, cohere, coherent, cohesive, hesitate, inherent
hetero-	different, other	heterogeneous, heterosexual
hex-	six	hexagon, hexahedron
hier-	sacred	hierarchy, hieroglyphics
hippo-	horse	hippodrome, hippopotamus
hole-	whole	holistic, hologram, holocaust
homo-, homeo-	same	homogeneous, homophone, homonym, homosexual, homeostasis, homeopathy
hore-	boundary	aphorism, horizon
hosp-/host-	host	hospice, hospital, hospitality, hostage, hostile
hume-, home-	ground, earth	exhume, Homo Sapiens, homicide, human, humane, humanity, humiliate, humus
hydr-	water	dehydrate, hydrant, hydraulics, hydrous
hypo-	under	hypothermia, hypochondria
hyper-	above, over	hyperbole, hypertonic
hypn-	sleep	hypnosis, hypnotherapy, hypnotise
iatr-	doctor	iatrogenic, psychiatrist
ide-	idea, thought	ideogram, idea, ideology
idio-	own, peculiarity	idiolect, idiom, idiopathic, idiosyncrasy, idiot
ign-	fire	igneous, ignite
imag-	copy	image, imagine
infra-	below, under	infrastructure, infrared (fracas)

Base	Denotation	Examples
insule-	island	insular, insulate, insulin, peninsula
ire-	anger, passion	irascible, irate, ire
iso-	equal, same	isobar, isometric, isosceles, isotonic
iter-	again	reiterate, iteration
jace-, ject-	cast, throw	adjacent, adjective, ejaculate, inject, object, project, reject, subject, trajectory
jane-	door	janitor, January
jude-, juse-, jure-	judge	adjudicate, judge, judicial, judiciary, jury, perjury
juge-	yoke	conjugal, jugular, subjugate, (conjunction)
juven-	young, youth	juvenile, rejuvenate
kilo-	thousand	kilobyte, kilogram, kilometre
kine-, cine-	movement, motion	cinema, kinaesthetic, kinetic, telekinesis
klept-	steal	kleptomania
labor-	work	collaboration, elaborate, laboratory
lact-	milk	lactate, lactation, lactose (galaxy)
lapid-	stone	dilapidate, lapidary (lapis lazuli)
late-	broad, wide	latitude, lateral
laud-	praise	laudable, laudanum
lave-	wash	lava, lavatory, lavender (laundry, lotion)
lax-	loose	laxative, relax
lege-, lect-	read, gather	collect, lecture, legend, legible, legion, privilege, religion, select (loyal)
lept-, leps-	grasp, seize	epilepsy, neuroleptic

Base	Denotation	Examples
leuc-, leuk-	white	leucocyte, leukaemia
luce-, lume-, lune-	light, brightness	Lucifer, lucid, luminous, lunar, lunatic
leve-	lift, light, raise	alleviate, elevate, lever, levity, levy, relieve
liber-	free	liberal, liberate, liberty
libr-	book	librarian, library
lige-	bind	ligament, ligature
lingu-	language, tongue	bilingual, linguine, linguistics (language)
liqu-	flow	liqueur, liquid, liquor
liter-	letter	alliteration, illiterate, literacy, literal, obliterate
lith-	stone	lithium, monolith, Neolithic, Palaeolithic
loce-	place	allocate, local, location, locomotion, locum
loge-	word, reason, speech, thought	analogy, apology, biology, dialogue, etymology, logarithm, logic, morphological, neologism, trilogy
loqu-, loc-	speak	colloquial, elocution, eloquent, soliloquy
lude-, luse-	play	allude, delude, elude, illusion, ludicrous
lysi-	dissolve	analysis, hydrolysis
macro-	long, large	macrobiotic, macroeconomics, macron
mag-, mega-, maj-, max	great, large	magnanimous, magnificent, magnify, magnum, major, majesty, megabyte, megalodon, maximum (much)
maj-	greater	majesty, major, mayor

Base	Denotation	Examples
mal-	bad, wretched	dismal, malady, malevolent, malfunction, malice
man-, main-	stay	mansion, permanent, remain
mane-	hand	emancipate, manacle, manage, manicure, manual, manuscript (mastiff)
mane-, ment-	think, mind	mania, mantra, comment, dementia, mental, mentality, mention (money)
mare-	sea	marinate, marine, maritime, marsh (meerkat)
mater-, matr-	mother	maternal, matrimony, matron
med-, -mid-	middle	immediate, intermediary, media, mediocre, medium, middle, midwife, midst (mean, Mesozoic)
mel-	honey	caramel, mellifluous (marmalade)
meme-	remember	commemorate, memoir, memory, remembrance (mourn)
mens-, metr-	measure	commensurate, dimension, immense, metric, symmetry
merc-	reward, wages, hire	commerce, commercial, merchant, mercy (market)
meta-	above, among, beyond	metabolism, metamorphosis, metaphor, method
meter-, metr-	measure	barometer, diameter, parameter, perimeter, thermometer
micro-	small	microcosm, microphone, microscope
milit-	soldier	militant, military, militia
mil-	thousand	millennium, million, millipede (mile)

Base	Denotation	Examples
mine-	less, smaller	minor, minuscule, minute, mince (mystery)
mir-	wonder, amazement	admire, miracle, mirror
mise-	hate	misandry, misanthropy, misogyny
miser-	unhappy, wretched	commiseration, miser, miserable
mis-, mit-	send	commit, emit, missile, mission, omit, permit, submit, transmit
mito-	thread	mitochondrion, mitosis
mne-	memory	amnesia, amnesty, mnemonic
mode-	measure, change	accommodate, mode, model, moderate, moderation, modern, modify
mone-	small, isolated	monarchy, monastery, monogram, monolith, monopoly, monotony
more-	foolish, dull	moron, oxymoron, sophomore
mord-, mors-	bite	mordacious, morsel, remorse
morph-	form, shape	endomorph, metamorphosis, morpheme
mort-	death	immortal, morbid, mortal, mortuary (mare)
mote-, move-	to push away	commotion, emotion, mobile, momentum, motion, motive, motor, move
multi-	many, much	multilingual, multiple, multiplex, multitude
mute-	change	immutable, mutation
my-	shut (the eyes)	myopia, mystery (mute)
myth-	story	mythology

Base	Denotation	Examples
narc-	numb	narcolepsy, narcotic, narcissist
nas-, nate-	born	innate, nascent, natal, native
nau-, naut-, nave-	ship	Argonaut, astronaut, nautical, navigate, navy, naufragous
neo-	new	neologism, neon, neophyte
nebul-	cloud	nebula, nebulous (Neptune)
necro-	dead	necrophobia, necrosis (nectar, nuisance)
nect-, nex-	join, tie	connect, nexus, annex (noose)
ne-, neg-	say no	negative, neglect, neuter, never, abnegate, (annihilate)
neuro-	nerve	neurology, neuron, neurotic
noce-, nox-	hurt, harm	innocent, innocuous, noxious
noct-, nox-	night	equinox, nocturnal
nome-	arrangement, law, order	astronomy, autonomous, economy, metronome, taxonomy (numb)
nomen-, nomin-, onym-	name	nomenclature, nominate, ignominy, anonymous, homonym (noun)
nove-	new	innovate, innovation, nova, novel, novice, renovate
nube-, nupt-	to marry, to wed	connubial, nubile, prenuptial (nymph)
nucle-	nut, kernel	nuclear, nucleus
numer-	number	enumerate, innumerable, numeral
nutri-	nourish	malnutrition, nutrient
oct-	eight	octagon, octopus, October
ode-	path, way	anode, diode, exodus, odometer

Base	Denotation	Examples
onto-	existing	ontogeny, ontology
oper-	work	cooperate, opera, operate, (opus)
opt-	choose	adopt, co-opt, optional
ore-	mouth	oral, orifice, adore
ord-	order	ordinal, ordinary, primordial
ortho-	straight	orthodontist, orthodox, orthopaedic
ove-	egg	oval, ovary, oviparous, ovule
paed- (US ped-)	child	paediatric, pedagogy
pal(a)eo-	old	Palaeozoic, palaeontology
pal-	be pale	pale, pallid, pallor, palomino (polio)
palp-	touch	palp, palpable, palpate, palpitation
pan-	all	panacea, pandemic, pandemonium, panoply
para- (1)	beside, near	parable, paradox, parallel, parameter, parody
para- (2)	protection against	parachute, parapet, parasol
pau-	little	paucity, Paul, pauper
pa-	feed	company, pastor, pasture, repast, pantry (foster)
path-	feeling, disease	apathy, empathy, pathetic, pathogen, sympathy
pater-, patr-	father	paternity, patriot, patron
pati-, pass-	suffer, feel, endure, permit	passion, passive, patience
pec-	sin	impeccable, peccadillo

Base	Denotation	Examples
pecu-	property	peculiar, pecuniary, pecunious
pede-, pode-	foot	centipede, impede, pedal, pedestrian, podium, arthropod
pel-, pulse-	drive, push	compel, dispel, expel, propulsion, pulse, repulsive
pene-	almost	peninsula, penultimate, penumbra
pene-, pune-	punish	impunity, penalty, penance, punish, (repent)
pend-, pens-	hang	pendant, pending, pendulum, pensive, suspense
pent-	five	pentagon, pentagram
peps-, pept-	digest	dyspepsia, peptic, peptide
pete-	strive toward, fly	appetite, compete, competition, impetus, petition (symptom)
phage-	eat	phagocyte, sarcophagus
pharmac-	drug, medicine	pharmaceuticals, pharmacy, pharmacology
phan-, phas-, phen-	to show, visible	emphasis, epiphany, phenomenon, sycophant (fantasy)
pher-, phor-	bear, carry	metaphor, pheromone
phile-	love, friendship	bibliophile, philanthropy, philharmonic, philosophy
phobe-	fear	claustrophobia, hydrophobia, agoraphobe, arachnophobia
phone-	sound	homophone, microphone, phonetic, phonics
photo-	light	photogenic, photograph

Base	Denotation	Examples
pi-	kind, devout	expiate, piety, pious, pity
pil-	hair	depilation, caterpillar
pisc-	fish	Pisces, piscine
place-	calm	implacable, placate
plane-	flat	explanation, planar, plane
plas-	mould	plasma, plastic
plate-	flat, broad	plateau, platitude, platypus (plaice)
plaud-, plause-	approve, clap	applaud, plaudit, plausible
ple-, plete-	fill	complement, complete, deplete, implement, supply
plene-	full	plenary, plenitude, plenty, replenish
plice-, plex-	fold	appliance, application, apply, complex, ply
pneu-	air, breath, lung	pneumatic, pneumonia (apnoea/apnea)
poe-	make, compose	poet, onomatopoeia
pole-	city	acropolis, cosmopolitan, metropolis, police, politics
poly-	many	polygamy, polygon
pone-, pose-	put	component, deposit, expose, position, positive, postpone, repose
popule-	people	population, popular, populous (people)
port-	carry	comportment, deport, export, import, port, portable, portal, porter, portfolio, rapport, report, support, transport
pot-	power	despot, potent, potential
pote-	drink	potable, potion

Base	Denotation	Examples
prece-	pray	deprecation, imprecation, precarious (pray)
prend-	grasp	apprehend, comprehend, comprehensive, enterprise, prehensile
prime-	first	primal, primary, prime, primeval, primitive
prive-	separate, take away	deprivation, privilege, privy
probe-, prove-	worthy, good	approbation, approve, reprobate (proof)
prop(e)r-	property, one's own	appropriate, proper, property, proprietary, proprietor, propriety
prox-	nearest	approximate, proximity (but not proxy!)
pseudo-	false	pseudonym, pseudopod
psych-	mind	psyche, psychiatry, psychology, psychosis
pter-	wing, feather	helicopter, pterodactyl
pude-	shame	impudent, repudiate
pugn-, pug-	fight	impugn, pugilism, pugnacious, repugnant (punch)
pung-, punct-	prick	acupuncture, expunge, punctual, punctuation, puncture, pungent
pupe-	doll	pupa, pupate, puppet
purge-	cleanse	expurgate, purgatory, purge
pute-	prune, reckon	amputation, compute, deputy, dispute, putative, reputation
quad-, quart-	four	quadrangle, quadrilateral, quadruped, quarter, quartile
quer-, quir-, quis-, ques	ask, seek	query, inquiry, inquisition, question

Base	Denotation	Examples
qui-	rest	acquit, quiet, requiem (while)
quote-	how many, how great	quota, quotient (quantity)
rade-, rase-	scrape, shave	abrade, erasure (rash, razor)
radi-	beam, spoke	radiance, radiation, radius
radic-	root	eradicate, radical, radish
ranc-	rancidness, grudge, bitterness	rancid, rancour
rege-, rex-, roy-	king	regal, regular, anorexia, royal (rule)
retro-	backward, behind	retrograde, retrospective, retrovirus
rhin-	nose, snout	rhinoceros, rhinoplasty
ride-, rise-	laugh	deride, ridiculous, risible
rode-, rose-	gnaw	corrode, erosion, rodent
roge-	ask	arrogant, derogatory, interrogation, surrogate
rube-	red	rubric, ruby
rude-	unskilled, rough, unlearned	erudite, rude, rudimentary
rupt-	break	abrupt, corrupt, disrupt, erupt, interrupt, rupture
sacr-	sacred	sacrament, sacred
sanct-	holy	sanctify, sanction, sanctuary
sapi-, sipi-	taste, wise	homo sapien, insipid, sapient
sarc-	flesh	sarcasm, sarcophagus
sati-	enough	sate, satisfy, saturate

Base	Denotation	Examples
scend-	climb	ascend, descend, transcendent
sci-	know	conscience, conscious, conscientious, science
scope-	look at, examine, view, observe	horoscope, kaleidoscope, microscope, periscope, sceptic
scribe-, script-	write	describe, manuscript, prescribe, scribble, scribe, script, scripture, subscribe
se-, sede-	apart, aside, away	secede, seditious, seduce
sect-, seg-	cut	section, segment
sede-, side-, sess-	sit	insidious, obsess, preside, president, reside, sedative, sediment, session, subside, supersede
sema-, semi-	sign	semantics, semaphore, semiotics
semi-	half	semicolon, semifinal
semin-	seed	insemination, seminal
sene-	old man	senator, senile, senior
sent-, sense-	feel	consensus, consent, dissent, resent, sense, sentence, sentient, sentiment
sequ-, sec-	follow	consecutive, consequence, prosecute, second, sequel (pursue)
sere-, sert-	join, line up	desert (to leave), insert, serial (exert)
serve-	save, protect, serve	conserve, reserve, service
sider-	star	consider, sidereal
sign-	sign	design, signal, signature, significant
simil-, semb-	likeness, imitating	assimilate, ensemble, resemble, simile, simulate, simulation, simultaneous

Base	Denotation	Examples
sist-	cause to stand (the letters <st> form many bases to do with standing)	assist, consist, desist, exist, insist, persist, resist
soci-	group	associate, social, society
sole- (1)	sun	solar, solstice
sole- (2)	comfort, soothe	consolation, console, solace
sole- (3)	alone, only	desolate, solitary, solo
sole- (4)	accustomed	insolent, obsolete
solve-, solu-	loosen, set free	absolute, absolve, soluble
some-	body	somatic, chromosome
somn-	sleep	insomnia, somnambulist, somnolent
sone-	sound	assonance, consonant, dissonance, resonance
soph-	wise	philosophy, sophism, sophisticated, sophomore
spect-, spic-	look	aspect, conspicuous, expect, inspect, species (Perspex)
spire-	breathe	aspire, conspire, expire, inspire, perspire, spirit
stel-	star	constellation, stellar
strate-	spread, strew	prostrate, stratify, stratus (street)
stil-	drip, drop	distillation, instil, still (for making alcohol)
strophe-	turning	apostrophe, catastrophe
struct-	to make up, build	construct, destruction, structure
sum-, sumpt-	take	assume, consume, presume

Base	Denotation	Examples
tace-, tice-	be silent	reticent, tacit, taciturn
tach-	swift	tachometer, tachycardia
tang-, ting-, tact-, tag-, tax-	touch, arrange	contact, contagious, contingent, contingency, tactile, tangible, taxidermy (dachshund)
tard-	slow	retardant, tardy
techn-	art, skill	technician, technology
tele-	far, end	telegram, television
temp-	time	contemporary, tempo, temporary
tome-	cut	anatomy, appendectomy, atom, dichotomy, tome
tene-, -tine-,	stretch	content, continue, tenacious, tenet, untenable (contain)
termin-	boundary, limit, end	determine, terminal, termination
ter-	earth	inter (v.), subterranean, terrace, terrarium, terrestrial, territory
test-	witness	attest, contest, detest, protest, testament, testify, testimony
text-	weave	context, pretext, textile, texture
the-	religion	atheist, pantheon, theology (enthusiasm)
therm-	heat, warm	thermal, hypothermia, thermometer
time-	frightened, shy	intimidate, timid, timorous
tope-	place	isotope, topiary, topic, utopia
torpe-	be numb	torpedo, torpid, torpor
torqu-, tort-	twist	contort, retort, torque, torture (truss)
tract-	draw, pull	attract, contract, subtract, tractor

Base	Denotation	Examples
tri-	three	triangle, tripod
tribe- (1)	rub	diatribe, tribulation
tribe- (2)	pay	contribute, retribution, tribute (tribe)
umbr-	shade, shadow	penumbra, umbrage, umbrella
uni-	one	union, unit, universe
und-	water, wave	abundant, redundant, undulate
urb-	city	suburb, urban
ute-, use-	use	abuse, use, usual, utility
vace-, vacu-	empty	evacuate, vacant, vacuum
vale-	strength, worth	equivalent, evaluate, valiant, valid, value
vanc-	empty, vain, idle	evanescent, vanity, vanish
vene-, vent-	come, go	adventure, avenue, convenient, event, venue
vere-	true	aver, veracious, verdict, verify, very
verb-	word	verb, verbatim, verbose
verse-, vert-	turn	adverse, avert, convert, diverse, divert, extrovert, universe, vertical
vest-	clothing, garment	divest, invest, vest
vi-	by way of	deviate, obviate, obvious, via
vice-	change	vicar, vice versa, vicissitude (weak)
vide-, vise-	see	evidence, provide, providence, video, vision, vista (envy)
vill-	house	villa, village, villain
vine-	wine	vinegar, vinyl, vine (wine)
vinc-, vict-	conquer	convict, convince, evict, vanquish, victory

Base	Denotation	Examples
vir-	man	triumvirate, virile
vite-, vive-	life	survive, viable, vital, vivacious, vivid, vivisection
vice-, vite-	fault, wickedness	vice, vicious, vitiate, vitiligo, vituperate
vitr-	glass	vitreous, vitriol, in-vitro
voce-	call, voice	advocate, vocal, vociferous
vol-	fly	volant, volatile, volley
vole-	will	benevolent, volunteer, voluptuous
volve-	roll	evolve, revolve (vault)
vore-	swallow	carnivore, voracious (devour)
vulge-	public	divulge, vulgar
xen-, xeno-	foreign, strange	xenophobia, xenon
xyl-	wood	xylophone, xylem, xylophagous
zo-	animal, living being	Mesozoic, protozoa, zodiac, zoo, Zoe

Appendix 3   Resources for everyone

Copy and laminate these word cards for use in test sentences.

Table A.1 Word cards

James	cat	idea
he	she	you
run	eat	slide
small	shiny	afraid
quickly	very	much

Mnemonics

Etymology

The mne- element denotes the mind, and interestingly resurfaces in *amnesia*.

Mnemonics now erase man's oldest nemesis: insufficient cerebral storage. (When converted to an acronym, this sentence spells *mnemonics*, but I don't think it's a particularly good mnemonic!)

Morphology and etymology are terrific tools for helping students study words in ways that reveal the underlying layers of the English writing system, and as a bridge to deeper and wider vocabulary building. This notion is being heartily embraced by educators the world over, much to the betterment of their students' linguistic output no doubt. However, as a 'good speller', I often examine the techniques I use to ensure that I write the correct letter sequences in complex words, and very often, I find that although morphology and etymology serve to *explain* those letter sequences, they don't always serve to *retrieve* those letter sequences when I need them. Instead, I use mnemonics. Similarly, when working with students on helping them achieve greater automaticity in writing, I often use a dual method of teaching the words we're studying by explaining the etymology, looking at their morphemes and related words etc, but also by showing them some memory hooks. This is a list of the ones I use frequently.

- **accommodation** 2 cottages and 2 mansions (how many <c>s and <m>s)
- **across** There's only one sea <c> to get across
- **address** You ADD your ADDress
- **affect/effect** Affect is the Action, effect is the rEsult
- **aggravate** Three angry *a's* and two growling *g's*
- **angle/angel** Angels have *gel* in their hair
- **ascertain** When you *ascertain* you need to be AS CERTAIN as you can
- **assassin** An assassin needs two donkeys—one to carry his guns and one to make a quick getaway. That's why he has two asses in his den (ASS ASS IN)
- **autumn/column/hymn/solemn** These words can be taught together with the sentence *He sang a solemn hymn between the columns in autumn.*
- **beautiful** Say the names of the first four letters very clearly while writing on the board. 'Beee-eeee-aaaaa-u-tiful!'
- **believe** You wouldn't *beLIEve* a LIE, would you?
- **biscuit** Breakfast Is Semi-Complete Unless I Taste *biscuits*
- **ceiling** Covers Everything Inside
- **colleague** The double *l* can be remembered by picturing two colleagues side by side
- **come/some** Taught together with *Rome, some*, and *home*: 'When we open the bird-cage, some fly to Rome and some come home'
- **complement/compliment** *ComplEment* adds something to make it Enough. A *compLIMEnt* puts you in the LIMElight. Taught together they are much easier to learn
- **currant/current** There is an ANT eating the currANT bun. So *currant* is the food and *current* is the flow
- **definitely** This word has *finite* in the middle. So often misspelled as 'definAtely'
- **desert** (like the Sahara) and **dessert** (like ice-cream), remember: the sweet one has two sugars (the letter *s* representing sugar)
- **diarrhoea** Dash In A Real Rush, Hurry Or Else Accident! (omit 'else' for US spelling)
- **disappoint** Don't disappoint your proud papa

- **eight** Every Insect Goes Home Tonight
- **embarrass** Two rosy red cheeks (the two R's in the middle) and two shy smiles (the two S's)
- **first** First Is Right before Second and Third
- **forty** Imagine a fairground for kids only. 'You can be four or fourteen, but u can't be forty!'
- **hear** You hEAR with your EAR
- **immediately** We ate immediATEly
- **island** An island IS LAND surrounded by water
- **laugh** Laugh And U Get Happy
- **leopard** Silent *o*, like the word *people*. 'When people see a leopard they say *o*!'
- **lose/loose** Lose lost an *o*
- **meat/meet** I like to eat meat
- **Mississippi** Say the letters out loud and you get an unforgettable rhythm. 'M . . . I . . . SS . . . I . . . SS . . . I . . . PP . . . I'
- **misspell** Imagine a very prim, old-style schoolmistress called Miss Pell. 'Miss Pell would never misspell'
- **necessary** Not Every Cat Eats Sardines – Some Are Really Yummy. And don't forget that the cat has one collar and two socks (one *c* and two *s*'s)
- **ocean** Only Crabs' Eyes Are Narrow
- **one** A small mouse lives alone in a big old abandoned house. He's lonely, and every night he can be heard calling for a friend in the huge, echoing dining room, 'Oh any *one*!' (Spell out the letters O-N-E and 1 as you say this)
- **other** 'That's my mother's other brother!' To which the response is 'O!'
- **our** Begin with the pronoun 'you', convert it to the possessive case by adding the suffix -r, then take away the <y>. Teach these together.
- **people** *See leopard*
- **pie** A PIEce of PIE
- **principal** The principal is your PAL
- **psychology** People Study You . . .
- **queue** There are two Ugly Elves in the queue (ue and ue). I remember this sequence by saying the letter names, i.e. <queue>
- **rhyme** Remember How You begin to RHYme
- **rhythm** *Activity:* 'Have you ever been really cheeky and said *Nyah-nyah-nyah-nyaaaaah-nyaaah!*'(Put your thumbs on your temples and waggle your fingers while you're saying it.) 'Well if you stand up and move your hips to the *rhythm* of that ever-so-cheeky statement, you'll cause much more offence!' (Have your students stand up and act this out.) This is because . . . Rhythm Helps Your Two Hips Move

- **said** Begin with *say, pay,* and *lay*. Show how the addition of the past tense suffix in all these words makes two things happen: The return of Illegal <i>, and the omission of the <e> in -ed.
- **secretary** Your SECRETary will keep your SECRET
- **separate** 'Separate me from that room! There's A RAT in it!'
- **sheriff** The sheriff has one rifle (one *r*) but fires twice (two *f's*)
- **temperature** Don't lose your TEMPER AT high temperatures
- **where** (As in *there* above) 'Where?' 'Here!'
- **which/witch** Which is a question word, just like *why, what, where, when, and who*, so it begins with the question grapheme <wh>. To remember the word *witch*, don't forget it's not a question word and she has a broomstick (the letter *t*)
- **you** 'Y-O-U spells *you*.' This is how my kids learned it
- **your** Adding *r* to show ownership, as in they + r → their
- **liaise** You must l i a i se with colleagues in Italy And Ireland
- **movable/moving** The *e* in move is very *movable* and disappears when you add a vowel suffix (but not a consonant suffix, such as *movement)*
- **parallel** Don't forget the *parallel* lines in the middle, but not at the end
- **parliament** The *ia* in the middle can be remembered thus: 'I AM a member of Parliament!'
- **scissors** A great way to remember this word is to mispronounce it, by saying the silent *c* — 'skissors'
- **stationery/stationary** You go to a baker, a butcher, a grocer – there's no question of the last two letters denoting their profession being 'er'. So it is with stationer—a person who provides stationEry.To go even further in the distinction—the suffix 'ary' denotes a state of being, such as primary, exemplary and of course, stationAry. I think you only need to explain the first to then derive the second, but as we know, there are no guarantees in life!
- **yacht** Yachts are costly, huge travellers

The months of the year

First some generalisations:

- There are three months of the year with a surprising letter *u*: JanUary, FebrUary, AugUst
- January and February both end with the same syllable *ary*

Then the tricky ones individually:

- **February** (Said in best Scottish accent) BR! Its FeBRuary in Scotland!
- **April** Don't be ILL in April (but leave the second L)

Non-spelling mnemonics

Long division

- Don't Miss The Bus.

  This stands for:

      Divide
      Multiply
      Take away
      Bring Down

- 7 basic roman numerals (I, V, X, L, C, D and M):

  M's 'mille' (or **1000** said)
  D's half (**500**—quickly read!)
  C's just a **100** (century!)
  and **L** is half again—**50**!
  So all that's left is **X** and **V**
  (or **10** and **5**)—and **I**—easy!

  Or . . .

  'Lucy **C**an't **D**rink **M**ilk'
  (L,C,D,M—50, 100, 500 and 1000)

- Measurement:

kilo-	hecto-	deca-	meter	deci-	centi-	milli-
x1000	x100	x10	1	1/10th	1/100th	1/1000th
Km	Hm	Dm	m	dm	cm	mm

  Remember: Killer Hound Dog Meets Deadly Cat Man

- Geography:

  Latitude 'Lat is Fat'—*Latitude* goes around the equator belt.

- The Colours of the Rainbow:

  Let us introduce our painter friend Roy G. Biv. He uses all the colours of the rainbow when he paints, that is, red, orange, yellow, green, blue, indigo, and violet.

- Music:

  Treble Clef: Lines from bottom up: Every Good Boy Deserves Fudge.
  Treble Clef: Spaces from bottom up: F-A-C-E.
  God is in Heaven – top space (G) and the Devil is in Hell – bottom space (D).
  Bass Clef: Lines from bottom up: Good Boys Deserve Fudge Always.
  Bass Clef: Spaces from bottom up: All Cows Eat Grass.
  Birds in the Sky – top space (B) and Fish in the Sea – bottom space (F).

- The days of the week:

  When learned together, the days of the week are much easier to spell as they can be associated with each other.

  First, the 'er' sounds in the days of the week are spelled *ur:* Sat**ur**day and Th**ur**sday. From there we can link Thursday to Tuesday as they both begin with *t* and have *u* in the first syllable. Then we introduce the fact that the days of the week are named after ancient Germanic gods and heavenly bodies.

  Monday is named after the moon.
  Tuesday was originally Tyr's day (the god of war).
  Wednesday, which should be sounded out as 'Wed-nes-day' was the god Woden (also known as Odin)'s day. He was the chief of the gods.
  Thursday is Thor's day (the god of thunder).
  Friday, on which (friends fry food, see *friend*) was Fryga's day. She was the goddess of love.
  Saturday is named after the planet Saturn.
  Sunday is named after the sun.

Glossary

Adjective A word which modifies a noun.

Adverb A word which modifies verbs, adjectives and other modifiers, phrases, and clauses.

Affix A letter or letters attached to a base to alter the base's meaning. From *ad-* 'to' + *fix* 'fasten'.

Alphabetic principle The understanding that speech can be turned into print and that print can be turned into speech.

Anglophone English-speaking. There are several varieties of English, including American English, British English, Australian English, Canadian English, South African English. There are also many sub-varieties of English, spoken as a first language in Jamaica, the Falkland Islands, Gibraltar, Anguilla and Saint Helena, to name but a few.

Auxiliary verb A word from a closed set that accompanies a main verb to help it express such things as tense and voice.

Case A form of a noun, pronoun, or adjective to show its relationship to other words, e.g. the pronoun *you* is expressed in the possessive case by using *your*.

Clause Any syntactic unit whose structure is, or is seen as reduced from, that of a sentence. Thus, in particular, one which includes a verb and the elements that accompany it.

Closed set A category of words with a small, unchanging membership.

Constituent A word or group of words that go together to form a unit and can be replaced by a single word.

Determiner Words which come before and limit a noun phrase. The most common determiners in English are the indefinite article *the* and the definite article *a/an*. The view in this book is that pronouns, such as *my, you, those,* etc., are also determiners.

Dialect The word choice, use, and pronunciation exclusive to a particular geographical region or social/professional group. The Australian dialect differs from the English dialect in numerous ways. These dialects can be categorised into further sub-dialects. People from Tasmania have a different word choice and pronunciation to people from Queensland, but they are both distinctively different Australian dialects.

Grammar The way in which words and sentences are constructed, according to certain rules, so that people can understand one another.

Idiolect The unique speech habits, including vocabulary, pronunciation, and word usage, that every human develops and uses.

Intransitive verb Verbs that do not have a direct object. Shown as *vi.* in dictionaries. Examples: sneeze, expire, etc. (see Intransitive verbs list in Verbs chapter).

Lexicon The unique store of words possessed by an individual.

Linguistics The systematic and scientific study of the structure of language. Linguistics can be described as dealing with three basic subjects: *phonetics and phonology* (the study of human speech sounds*), syntax* (the study of sentence structure), *semantics and pragmatics* (the study of logic and meaning).

Main verb The verb that carries the semantic content. The *meaning* verb, as opposed to the auxiliary verb that gives any old verb its tense.

Modifier A word which adds meaning or colour to another word. Traditionally these are known as adjectives and adverbs but can also incorporate possessive pronouns, number words and determiners.

Morpheme A minimal unit of grammatical structure. 'Eating' has two morphemes, the root word 'eat' and the suffix '-ing'.

Neologism A new word invented through slang usage or jargon which has caught on and is in use in a group of people.

Object The noun in a sentence which receives the energy of a verb. E.g. *I like cats*, in which the noun *cats* receives my liking.

Open set A class of words that frequently acquires new members. Nouns, verbs, and adjectives are open-set words. New coinages are adding to the list of these words continually.

Parsing The task of assigning words to their parts of speech.

Parts of speech Also known as *word classes* or *lexical categories*. The names we give words based on how they are used and how they relate to other words in utterances.

Phoneme The smallest possible unit of sound. The word 'pat' has three phonemes, in that it can be broken into three separate units. The word 'path' also has three phonemes, the units /p-a-th/.

Phonemic awareness The ability to perceive the number, order, sameness, and difference of individual sounds within words.

Phonology The study of the sound system of a language and the relationships within.

Phrase Any group of words that is not a clause but can function as a whole in a larger utterance.

Preposition A word which connects a preceding noun or verb to a following noun.

Pronoun A word which stands for or makes you think of nouns or noun phrases.

Register The variety of language used according to the perceived social setting, ranging from formal to informal.

Semantics In linguistics, the study of logic and meaning.

Sentence A group of words which expresses a complete thought, having a subject (either apparent or implied) and a verb.

Standard A form of language used as a measure or model for comparison.

Standardisation The formation of agreed standards of a language.

Subject The part of the sentence that is performing the action of the verb.

Suffix An element placed at the end of a base with the purpose of changing the base's meaning.

Syllable A unit of sound produced with one impulse of the voice.

Syntax The study of grammatical relations between words and other units within the sentence.

Tense The time of an event in relation to the time of speaking. In English, verbs are used to show tense.

Transitive verb A verb which has an object. In sentence *The mice ate the cheese*, the verb *ate* is transitive, as it carries the action of eating straight to the cheese.

Utterance Thing which is said without interruption, either in speech or writing.

Voice A verb's form that shows how it is related to the subject. Most recognisable are active and passive voice. The verb *ate* in *The mice ate the cheese* is active. If we were to make *cheese* the subject of the sentence, then the verb would have to change its form to passive voice: *The cheese was eaten by the mice.*

Word Grammar Model of grammar developed in the 1980s by R. A. Hudson. Word Grammar has provided the chief inspiration for the units on the parts of speech in this book.

Bibliography

Bowers, P. N., Kirby, J. R., & Deacon, S. H. (2010). The effects of morphological instruction on literacy skills: A systematic review of the literature. *Review of Educational Research, 80*(2), 144–179.

Bryson, B. (1990). *Mother tongue*. London: Penguin.

Bullock, A. (1975). A language for life (1st edn). London: Her Majesty's Stationery Office.

Carstairs-McCarthy, A. (2018). *An introduction to English morphology: Words and their structure* (2nd edn). Edinburgh: Edinburgh University Press.

Cavalli, E., Colé, P., Badier, J.-M., Zielinski, C., Chanoine, V., & Ziegler, J. (2016). Spatiotemporal dynamics of morphological processing in visual word recognition. *Journal of Cognitive Neuroscience, 28*(8), 1228e1242.

The Concise Oxford English Dictionary (1999). Oxford: Clarendon Press.

Cran, W., MacNeil, R., & McCrum, R. (1986). *The story of English.* London: Faber and Faber.

Crystal, D. (1974). *What is linguistics?* London: Edward Arnold.

Crystal, D. (1976). *Child language, learning and linguistics*. London: Edward Arnold.

Crystal, D. (2006). *The fight for English*. Oxford: Oxford University Press.

Crystal, D. (2008). '2b or not 2b?' *The Guardian*, 5 July. https://www.theguardian.com/books/2008/jul/05/saturdayreviewsfeatres.guardianreview

Denham, K., & Lobeck, A. (eds) (2010). *Linguistics at school*. Cambridge: Cambridge University Press.

The Economist style guide (2005). London: Profile Books.

Ellis, A. W. (1993). *Reading, writing and dyslexia: A cognitive analysis* (2nd edn). Hove, UK: Lawrence Erlbaum.

Engelmann, S., Haddox, P., & Bruner, E. (1983). *How to teach your child to read in 100 easy lessons*. New York: Simon and Schuster.

Graven, S., & Browne, J. (2008). Auditory development in the fetus and infant. *Newborn & Infant Nursing Reviews, 8*(4), 187.

Haegeman, L. (1991). *Introduction to government and binding theory*. Oxford: Blackwell Publishers.

Hattie, J., & Yates, G. (2014). *Visible learning and the science of how we learn*. Oxford: Routledge.

Heffer, S. (2014). *Simply English*. London: Random House.

Higbee, K. L. (1996). *Your memory: How it works and how to improve it* (2nd edn). Cambridge, MA: Da Capo Press.

Hochman, J., Wexler, N., & Lemov, D. (2017). *The writing revolution: A guide to advancing thinking through writing in all subjects and grades*. Hoboken NJ: Jossey-Bass a Wiley Brand.

Hudson, R. (1981). 83 things linguists can agree about, *Journal of Linguistics, 17*, 179.

Hudson, R. (2010). *An introduction to word grammar*. Cambridge: Cambridge University Press.

Kamm, O. (2015). *Accidence will happen: The non-pedantic guide to English usage*. London: Weidenfeld & Nicolson.

Labov, W. (1994). *Principles of linguistic change, internal factors*. Massachusetts: Blackwell.

Liberman, A. (2005). *Word origins . . . and how we know them: Etymology for everyone*. Oxford: Oxford University Press.

Matthews, P. H. (1997). *The Oxford concise dictionary of linguistics*. Oxford: Oxford University Press.

Murray, D. (1998). Ebonics: A case study in language, power, and pedagogy. *TESOL Quarterly, 32*(1), 144–146.

Nagy, W., & Anderson, R.C. (1984). How many words are there in printed school English? *Reading Research Quarterly, 19*, 304–330.

Nagy, W., Anderson, R., Schommer, M., Scott, J., & Stallman, A. (1989). Morphological word families in the internal lexicon. *Reading Research Quarterly, 24*, 262–282.

Pinker, S. (1994). *The language instinct*. New York: Penguin.

Pinker, S. (1997). *How the mind works*. New York: Penguin.

Pinker, S. (2014). *The sense of style*. New York: Penguin.

Rastle, K. (2019). The place of morphology in learning to read in English. *Cortex, 116*, 45–54.

Scibetta Hegland, S. (2021). *Beneath the surface of words*. Sioux Falls: Learning About Spelling.

Shillcock, R., & Monaghan, P. (2003). *An anatomical perspective on sublexical units*: The influence of the split fovea. Edinburgh: University of Edinburgh.

Smith, A., & Kim, S. (2017). *This language, a river*. Peterborough, ON: Broadview Press.

Smith, N. (1989). *The Twitter machine*. Oxford and Massachusetts, MA: Blackwell.

Sweller, J., Ayres, P., & Kalyuga, S. (2020). *Cognitive load theory Vol. 1*. New York: Springer.

UK Parliament. House of Lords. (1979). *Parliamentary debates (Hansard)*. https://hansard.parliament.uk/lords/1979-11-21/debates/4465a0a3-5112-40d5-91bd-a0bf8ecba53f/TheEnglishLanguageDeteriorationInUsage

Trask, R. L. (1996). *A dictionary of phonetics and phonology*. London: Routledge.

Truss, L. (2003). *Eats, shoots & leaves: The zero tolerance approach to punctuation*. New York: Gotham Books.

Venable, G. (2021). *Backpocket words*. San Francisco: One Monkey Books.

Westwood, P. (1997). *Commonsense methods for children with special needs* (3rd edn). London and New York: Routledge.

Willingham, D., & Lovette, G. (2014). Can reading comprehension be taught? *Teachers College Record*, 26 September.

Index